Also by John Ashbery

FLOW CHART

FLOW CHART

JOHN ASHBERY

Alfred A. Knopf   New York   1991

THIS IS A BORZOI BOOK
PUBLISHED BY ALFRED A. KNOPF, INC.

Selections from this poem have appeared in *American
Poetry Review*, *o·blēk*, *The Paris Review*, and *Scripsi*.

The author is grateful to the John D. and Catherine
T. MacArthur Foundation for a fellowship that was
of great help in writing this book.

Library of Congress Cataloging-in-Publication Data
Ashbery, John.
Flow chart / John Ashbery. — 1st ed.
p.   cm.
ISBN 0–679–40201–2
I. Title.
PS3501.S475F5   1991
811'.54—dc20   90–52903   CIP

Manufactured in the United States of America

FIRST EDITION

for David

FLOW CHART

Still in the published city but not yet
overtaken by a new form of despair, I ask
the diagram: is it the foretaste of pain
it might easily be? Or an emptiness
so sudden it leaves the girders
whanging in the absence of wind,
the sky milk-blue and astringent? We know life is so busy,
but a larger activity shrouds it, and this is something
we can never feel, except occasionally, in small signs
put up to warn us and as soon expunged, in part
or wholly.
          Sad grows the river god as he oars past us
downstream without our knowing him: for if, he reasons,
he can be overlooked, then to know him would be to eat him,
ingest the name he carries through time to set down
finally, on a strand of rotted hulks. And those who sense something
squeamish in his arrival know enough not to look up
from the page they are reading, the plaited lines that extend
like a bronze chain into eternity.
                    It seems I was reading something;
I have forgotten the sense of it or what the small
role of the central poem made me want to feel. No matter.

The words, distant now, and mitred, glint. Yet not one
ever escapes the forest of agony and pleasure that keeps them
in a solution that has become permanent through inertia. The force
of meaning never extrudes. And the insects,
of course, don't mind. I think it was at that moment he
knowingly and in my own interests took back from me
the slow-flowing idea of flight, now
too firmly channeled, its omnipresent reminders etched
too deeply into my forehead, its crass grievances and greetings
a class apart from the wonders every man feels,
whether alone in bed, or with a lover, or beached
with the shells on some atoll (and if solitude
swallow us up betimes, it is only later that
the idea of its permanence sifts into view, yea
later and perhaps only occasionally, and only much later
stands from dawn to dusk, just as the plaintive sound
of the harp of the waves is always there as a backdrop
to conversation and conversion, even when
most forgotten) and cannot make sense of them, but he knows
the familiar, unmistakable thing, and that gives him courage
as day expires and evening marshals its hosts, in preparation
for the long night to come.
                         And the horoscopes flung back
all we had meant to keep there: *our* meaning, for us, yet
how different the sense when another speaks it!
How cold the afterthought that takes us out of time
for a few moments (just as we were beginning to go with the fragile
penchants mother-love taught us) and transports us to a stepping-stone
far out at sea.
              So no matter what the restrictions, admonitions,
premonitions that trellised us early, supporting this

artificial espaliered thing we have become, by the same token no
subsequent learning shall deprive us, it seems, no holy
sophistication loosen the bands
of blessed decorum, our present salvation, our hope for years to come.
Only let that river not beseech its banks too closely,
abrade and swamp its levees, for though the flood is always terrible,
much worse are the painted monsters born later
out of the swift-flowing alluvial mud.
                                    And when the time for the breaking
of the law is here, be sure it is to take place in the matrix
of our everyday thoughts and fantasies, our wonderment
at how we got from there to here. In the unlashed eye of noon
these and other terrible things are written, yet it seems
at the time as mild as soughing of wavelets in a reservoir.
Only the belated certainty comes to matter much,
I suppose, and, when it does, comes to seem as immutable as roses.
Meanwhile a god has bungled it again.
                                    Early on
was a time of seeming: golden eggs that hatched
into regrets, a snowflake whose kiss burned like an enchanter's
poison; yet it all seemed good in the growing dawn.
The breeze that always nurtures us (no matter how dry,
how filled with complaints about time and the weather the air)
pointed out a way that diverged from the true way without negating it,
to arrive at the same result by different spells,
so that no one was wiser for knowing the way we had grown,
almost unconsciously, into a cube of grace that was to be
a permanent shelter. Let the book end there, some few
said, but that was of course impossible; the growth must persist
into areas darkened and dangerous, undermined
by the curse of that death breeze, until one is handed a skull

as a birthday present, and each closing paragraph of the novella is
underlined: *To be continued,* that there should be no peace
in the present, no sleep save in glimpses of the future
on the crystal ball's thick, bubble-like surface. No you and me
unless we are together. Only then does he mumble confused words
of affection at us as the barberry bleeds close against the frost,
a scarlet innocence, confused miracle, to us, for what we have done
to others, and to ourselves. There is no parting. There is
only the fading, guaranteed by the label, which lasts forever.

This much the gods divulged before they became too restless,
too preoccupied with other cares to see into the sole fact the
present allows, along with much ribbon, much icing
and pretended music. But we can't live with them in their day:
the air, though pure, is too dense. And afterwards when others
come up and ask, what was it like, one is too amazed to behave strangely;
the future is extinguished; the world's colored paths all lead
to my mouth, and I drop, humbled, eating from the red-clay floor.
And only then does inspiration come: late, yet never too late.

It's possible, it's just possible, that the god's claims
fly out windows as soon as they are opened, are erased from the accounting. If
    one is alone,
it matters less than to others embarked on a casual voyage
into the promiscuity of dreams. Yet I am always the first to know
how he feels. The inventory of the silent auction
doesn't promise much: one chewed cactus, an air mattress,

a verbatim report. Sandals. The massive transcriptions with which
he took unforgivable liberties—hell, I'd sooner join the project
farther ahead, retaining all benefits, but one is doomed,
repeating oneself, never to repeat oneself, you know what I mean?
If in the interval false accounts have circulated, why,
one is at least unaware of it, and can live one's allotted arc
of time in feasible unconsciousness, watching the linen dresses of girls,
with a wreath of smoke to come home to. There is nothing beside the familiar
doormat to get excited about, yet when one goes out in loose weather
the change is akin to choirs singing in a distance nebulous with fear
and love. Sometimes one's own hopes are realized
and life becomes a description of every second of the time it took;
conversely, some are put off by the sound of legions milling about.
One cultivates certain smells, is afraid to leave the charmed circle
of the anxious room lest uncommitted atmosphere befall

and the oaks

are seen to be girdled with ivy.

Alack he said what stressful sounds

More of him another time but now you
in the ivory frame have stripped yourself one by one of your earliest
opinions, polluted in any case by bees, and stand
radiant in the circle of our lost, unhappy youth, oh my
friend that knew me before I knew you, and when you came to me
knew it was forever, *here* there would be no break, only I was
so ignorant I forgot what it was all about. You chided me

for forgetting and in an instant I remembered everything: the
schoolhouse, the tent meeting. And I came closer until the day
I wrote my name firmly on the ruled page: that was a
time to come, and all happy crying in memory placed the stone
in the magic box and covered it with wallpaper. It seemed our separate
lives could continue separately for themselves and shine like a single star.
I never knew such happiness. I never knew such happiness could exist.
Not that the dark world was removed or brightened, but
each thing in it was slightly enlarged, and in so seeming became its
true cameo self, a liquid thing, to be held in the hollow
of the hand like a bird. More formal times would come
of course but the abstract good sense would never drown in the elixir
of this private sorrow, that would always sing to itself
in good times and bad, an example to one's consciousness,
an emblem of correct behavior, in darkness or under water.
How unshifting those secret times, and how stealthily
they grew! It was going to take forever just to get through
the first act, yet the scenery, a square of medieval houses, gardens
with huge blue and red flowers and solemn birds that dwarfed
the trees they sat on, need never have given way to the fumes and crevasses
of the high glen: the point is one was going to do to it
what mattered to us, and all would be correct as in a painting
that would never ache for a frame but dream on as nonchalantly as we did.
Who could have expected a dream like this to go away for there are some
that are the web on which our waking life is painstakingly elaborated:
there are real, bustling things there and the burgomaster of success
stalks back and forth, directing everything
with a small motion of a finger. But when it did come,
the denouement, we were off drinking in some restaurant,
too absorbed, too eternally, expectantly happy to be there or care.

§

That inspiration came later, in sleep while it rained,
urgently, so that lines of darkness interfered with the careful
arrangement of the dream's disguise: no takers? Anyway,
sleep itself became this chasm of repeated words,
of shifting banks of words rising like steam
out of someplace into something. Forget the promises the stars made you: they
    were half-stoned, and besides
are twinned to no notion that can have an impact
on our way of thinking, as crabbed now
as at any time in the past. A forlorn park stood before us
but there was no way to want to enter it, since the guards
had abandoned their posts to slate-gray daylight
flowing into your heart as though it were a blotter, confounding
or negating the rare survival of wit into our century:
these, at any rate, are my children, she intoned,
of whom I divest myself so as to fit into the notch
of infinity as defined by a long arc of crows returning to the distant
coppice. All's aglow. But we see by it that some mortal
material was included in the glorious compound, that next to
nothing can prevent its mudslide from sweeping over us
while it renders the pitted earth smooth and pristine and something
like one's original idea of it, only so primitive
it can't understand us. Meanwhile the coat I wear,
woven of consumer products, asks you to pause and inspect
the still-fertile ground of our once-valid compact
with the ordinary and the true. It wants out and
we shall get it even with decreased services and an increased

number of spot-checks, since all of it, ourselves included,
is in our own interests to speak up for and deny when the proper
moment arrives. Now, nothing further remains to be done except
to sleep and pray, saving the pieces for a slightly
later time when they shall be recognized as holy remnants of the burnished
mirror in which the Almighty once saw Himself, and wept,
realizing how all His prophecies had come true for His people
at last and no one was any wiser for it as they walked the wide
shadowless streets with no eyelids or memory when it came to
intersecting the itineraries of other, similarly blessed creatures
(blessed for having no name, no preconceived strategies
unless they lay underground, too unprofitable to dig up
until the requisite technologies had been developed some
decades down the road and nodding as though in acknowledgment of
an acquaintance one doesn't remember yet is not sure of
having ever formally renounced either: was it on land or at sea
that that bird first came to one, many miles from the nearest anything?).

What we are to each other is both less urgent and more
perturbing, having no discernible root, no raison d'être, or else flowing
backward into an origin like the primordial soup it's so easy to pin
anything on, like a carnation to one's lapel. So it seems we must
stay in an uneasy relationship, not quite fitting
together, not precisely friends or lovers though certainly not enemies, if
the buoyancy of the spongy terrain on which we exist is to be experienced
as an ichor, not a commentary on all that is missing from the reflection
in the mirror. *Did I say that? Can this be me?* Otherwise the treaty will
seem premature, the peace unearned, and one might as well slink back
into the solitude of the kennel, for the blunder to be read as anything

but willful, self-indulgent. And meanwhile everything around us is already
prepared for this resolution; the temperature, the season are exactly right
for it all not to be awash with sentiments expelled from some impossibly
distant situation; some episode from your childhood nobody knows about and
even you can't remember accurately. It is time for the long beds
then, and the extra hours to be spent in them, but surely somebody can
find something spontaneous to say before it all fizzles, before the incandescent
tongs are slaked in mud and the tender yellow shoots of the willow
dry up instead of maturing having concluded that the moment
is inappropriate, the heroes gone to their rest, and all the plain
folk of history foundered in the subjective reading of their lives
as expendable, the stuff of ordinary heresy, shards of common crockery
interesting only because unearthed long after the time had come for a
decision on what to do at the very moment they disappeared into timelessness,
one of innumerable such tramping exits that no one hears,
so long as they may be promptly and justly forgotten,
subtracted like the soul we never knew we had and replaced with something
young, and easier, climate of any day and of all the days, postmillenarian.

Just so, some argue, some still are
nurtured by their innocence, a wanton
formula a nursemaid gives them. They grow up to be slim,
and tall, but often it seems something is lacking,
some point of concentration around which a person can collect itself,
and be neither conscious nor uncaring, be neutral.
And when the pitcher
is emptied of milk, it is not refilled, but washed and put away on a shelf.
Conversations are still initiated,
haltingly, under the leaves, around an outdoor table,

but they insist on nothing and are remembered
only as disquieting examples of how life might be
in that other halting yet prosperous time
when games of strength were put away.
And each guest rises
abruptly from the table, a star at his or her shoulder.
For then, in smeared night, no blotch or defect can erase it,
the wonderful greeting you heard in the morning
and heard yourself reply to.

But at times such as
these late ones, a moaning in copper beeches is heard, of regret,
not for what happened, or even for what could conceivably have happened, but
for what never happened and which therefore exists, as dark
and transparent as a dream. A dream from nowhere. A dream
with no place to go, all dressed up with no place to go, that an axe
menaces, off and on, throughout eternity. Or ships, lands
which no one sees, islands scattered like pebbles
across the immense surface of the ocean; this is what it is
to believe and not see, to implore dreaming, then to arrive home
by cunning, stricken and exhausted, a framed picture of oneself. The ads
didn't tell you this, they were too busy with their own professional sleight-of-
    hand
to notice those farther out in deep water (*"when such a destin'd wretch
as I, wash'd headlong from on board"*), decorating the maelstrom with
someone's (I wish I knew whose) notion of what is right, or cute.
Soon the dark chairs and tables stand out sharply in front of strange
green-striped walls, gulls circle in the sky, smoke
from piles of old tires set alight at strategic points throughout the city

sifts through the crack where the pane doesn't quite join the sill—
is this, I ask you, a mute entreaty on the part of some well-intentioned
but shy deity meant to take the temperature of the lives being squandered
by the few left here below? Ask, rather, why the clock slows down
a little more each day, necessitating double, triple and even quadruple
    tintinnabulations
in order for its fundamentally banal intentions to be elucidated
so that one may settle down to enjoying the usufruct of the sparse,
shattering seconds, the while looking forward to retiring at ninety
on a comfortable income without rueing the day one first took up the odd
gambit that has projected us into a lifetime of self-loathing and shallow interests.
One lives thus, plucking a mean sort of living from the rubbish heaps
of history, unaware that the parallel daintiness of the lives of the rich,
like fish in an ocean whose bottom is dotted with the rusted engines and debris
of long-forgotten wrecks, unfolds; yes, "*And I in greater depths than he,*" I
    suppose,
yet it doesn't help deliver one back either to the after all sane and helpful blank
    square
one is always setting out from, having in the meantime forgotten those other
precepts, sane and insane, that intrude as soon as one begins to think
about anything at all. It is always on the rim of some fleshpot briefly
mentioned in the Bible one is seen to squirm, a pinned worm, so that
one is pitted against others as against oneself: lonesome, hungry,
and a little bit thirsty until the day of doom universally misconstrued as a
time of relief and pillars of dust rising straight up out of the desert valleys
where one's feet take one, and all that mythology of broken tracks,
jettisoned equipment, and the long-uninhabited wadi whose watering-trough
is merely mud now and a few puddles of camel-stale, materializes.

§

Latest reports show that the government
still controls everything but that the location of the blond captive
has been pinpointed thanks to urgent needling from the backwoods constituency
and the population in general is alive and well. But can we dwell
on any of it? Our privacy ends where the clouds' begins, just here, just at
this bit of anonymity on the seashore. And we have the right
to be confirmed, just as animals or even plants do, provided we go away and leave
every essential piece of the architecture of us behind. Surely then, what we work
        for must be met
with approval sometime even though *we* haven't the right to issue any
such thing. There are caves and caves, and almost none
of them has been explored yet. That doesn't give us much
to go on, yet we insistently cry that someone else's rondo is already
being played, and that over and over, so how come nobody does anything about it,
relaxes us in our shoes and tells us about bedtime? Surely, in my younger
days people acted differently about it. There was no barnstorming, just quiet
people going about their business and not worrying too much about
being rewarded at the end when it came down to that. No, we were wandering
away, too busy for such things, toward the altar,
or better yet into the nave whose fruit-and-flower
decoration led unostentatiously and facilely into the outdoors it
anticipated. No use just sitting around juicing the lemon
or the orange for that matter as long as one was intending to get up and play
again. And now that the time of reckoning nears, it wears a changed coat;
its color is brighter. No but there must be some structural difference as well
in the ordering of the colors and how they were laid on, only
no one can conceivably care enough about this to talk about it. Well I do
and can, but the un-nice fractions almost always assert themselves
above the din of this great city and I have trouble remembering
even my name until some passing girl kindles its fancy, what my name was
to me when I first began to think about other things. There is not postage for

this boredom either really so that it keeps
returning, might be said never to have gone away at all,
except for the media with which it keeps getting compared. I say, the other
reaches really tickle you, when you have a chance. And all this time
I thought he was only farting around disinclined to have a serious opinion
on anything, and even more so to give it vent or utterance. And my sight clears
for the first time in a thousand years and it's true, I can see up ahead
where no one waits and the long flags flap and droop in the dust of sunsets
and so may it be forever and ever till we get it right. Mine's isn't the option to
show you how to escape or comfort you unduly but with a little time
and a little patience we shall make this thing work. Even though you thought
everything you touched was doomed to fall apart or not start, time has
a few surprises up its sleeve and deserves to be spat on for not having more,
or would, if it didn't. Yet it does. There are promises clad with the finest
silk you can imagine and silver ornaments hitherto undreamed of, if only you can
match them with something of equal loveliness and curiosity from your own
secret collection. And of course this does take time, but in the end one
senses it more richly bedizened than ever before, and in line for a promotion
out of the ranks of futility into the narrow furrows of bliss and total sublimity
crystallized in good humor that took over early on in the century. Of course,
no one is aware of this. Yet. But give
everybody time, even no-shows, and it will all flow backwards, that
caparisoned night, a trial for some, and otherwise it all gets out
into your childhood and the beach that was its launching pad before
hunger and fears took over even as delight fostered the notion that
there was going to be enough for everybody, for children to pause
and have a happy home no one talks about anymore. Best to rest, sleep and laugh
about it to someone who no longer matters and then you'll find that you are indeed
in it and have been all along, only that the show was on a kind of treadmill moving
at the same leaden pace as your jokes and ambitions, which is why you
never knew about it and therefore consented to come along anyway

on this dangerous outing to the very sources of time. Don't
excuse yourself, nothing could.

I've never really considered telling you. And now. He hated
doing it—he wasn't sure why. And so just as the mirthless sequel was being
disinterred, a feeling of rage came over him, but also of relief, because
you couldn't do it now. They're lost somewhere out there between the trees
and muck, besides all cars have them now. And the colorful glasses and telephone
are there; he came for a fitting. It was proper, and in its time. But no
matter what you do someone will be malevolent about it, and try to stop you,
though there is no stopping them. He came for the fitting and tried
it on and it fit, just like that. What a laugh. Oh yes she laughed out
of the closet I'll be there in a minute dear. You see
how fond of him she was, and he, well he just took it,
like most things, change, pretzels. And she thought he was
so good at it it kind of faked her when the last windshield whizzed
by and it was all over as though in a rush. And as meat is sung,
and lips only slowly parted for the alphabet of night chimes to come
clanging down like an immense ring of keys, so with the gale-
whipped morsel, notion of itself, that dogs us and all humans, and we never
quite get out from under it, there is always a thread of it attached to you
and when you remove that, another one as though magnetized takes its place.
Begorrah it was dumb to be in the pit with him, for then the sentence . . .
But who knows what all they may have tried before, what
avenues exhausted before it was time to mend and really be the interloper,
and for all its sparks it was never considered dangerous.
Everybody gets such ideas on occasion, but here was the little shot-glass
of night, all ready to drink, and you spread out in it
even before it radiates in you. It doesn't matter whether or not

you like the striations, because, in the time it takes to consider them,
they will have merged, the rich man's house become a kettle, the wreath
in the sink turned to something else, and still the potion holds,
prominent. And you want to see it and to have it be talked about this way,
not drool aimless compassion. So on that night we were almost boarded up,
packed off to a vacation—where? Moreover no men heard of it,
only teen-age girls and male adolescents with fruited complexions and scalps,
who were going to make it difficult for one should an occasion arise.

But a funny
thing happened, none of us were around to count, all incommensurate with our
duties as we should forever be, and not wanting much training. The dark
was like nectar that evening, rising in the mouth; you thought you had never heard
so pretty a sound. Then, of course, quietism was again broached
and that soon, and quite soon the pink of the salmon ignited the whey
of the plover's egg and the black of old, scarred metal; then, how it
feels relaxes one like a warm, numbing bath, and her argument, and yours,
and all of theirs—why, why not just consider, or better yet, just
hold, hold on to them? For the speed of light is far away,
and you, sooner or later, must return
to a deteriorated situation, and, placing your hand in the fire, say
just what it means to you to be connected
and over, and kiss the burning edges of the unfolded, stiff
card, and be unable to avoid doing anything about it or acknowledging it
when we have passed, when all is past.

And why did
he, by what was he it? Why, we push our little tales around
and back and forth and so on
by which time it literally *implodes*, I mean by then he was settling in
and no one called his attention to it. In your repertory of groans is one
glottal one—you'll feel the difference. And if it can't liberate itself from us,
just turns to dust in the air floating with the kind of negative majesty one thought

one would not see again in one's life. But I had the horn—we had a deal we
    agreed on, yet
no record of its existence is sketched, and I am all I am
in the meanwhile and 13,000 fucking miles away like a planter
on his porch. And so I am unaware of the flambeaux and, possibly, the stealth
that brought me here. And abandoned me—I—
I'm awfully sorry, big boy, but my plans concern George and his wife over by
    the other side
of the lake slipping into a nervous breakdown, and I, we, well as you know, we
sit here determined, not like the rind
of the melon but not liking to say anything about it into the miraculous dawn
that—gasp—gathers us into its stocking. A pervasive air about him of studious
lyricism avoided us, and he turned, ever so quickly, to the hen house, and off
in the open was seen running, and then, it's so easy, was probably not recorded
except between the trees of a clearing. And who, what patron saint, will pick up
the pieces of the glittering lighthouse and restore us to them in a kind
of Roman calm, that we were meant for? And suddenly SHIT it's the fire and
glass breaking everywhere—it's as though you were never born but you must
    somehow
drink a toast to the small nucleus of watch-springs or confusion that
lords it over you now but will be less than an unconsumed coal among ashes, soon,
until the dryer's fixed. And then all out and along the
cinder path that led so alluringly down to the bayou, all we can know is hope
and fevers for a coming tomorrow of saffron and moist rage under the corner
of someone's hat that wasn't meant to like you. Me, I
rest in the sun regardless. We saw a car drive on to the city that
is the password. Ice-cubes played tag up and down my spine. I'm
here to collect the reward. Obey my every command, no matter
how strange it may seem, otherwise we'll have been banished before the
    judgment,
not know how fortunate we were in our old simplicity. Other vanished

zinnias were interviewed and nobody had anything, good or bad, to say about us,
which doesn't cause any tears yet one wonders: what if one *were* back there again?
On whom might one rely? What distractions would be concocted for us
if we had strayed? And who is the baron that manipulates our daily lives
from afar? Why even depend on industry and innocence when rebellion is
    growing
in the ditch just outside? Who knows about us? Who ever did? Weren't we
lying to ourselves when we thought we caught someone being just slightly
interested in us one day, and if so, whose fault is it? That we came
too late to an overgrown baseball diamond? And in the meantime shacks had
    vanished
without a trace from the face of the globe
and now the evening star was combing her hair at the attic window
and no one is to blame, just be calm, don't
rush, it's all over or soon will be or just was, in any
other language sufficient to tell it in—just like it was.

It has long been my contention that jackals,
unlike other denizens of the epistemic forest, are able to predict
the future of metabolizing some kind of parasite that grows on other people's
children and devours them. The eyes are a profound cobalt blue, accepting
of moral dilemmas and sprouting proverbs
slowly, like crystals,
but no, not innocent,
and not lacking in character. Twenty years ago, you will recall, the eyes
thought they made a difference, were glazed, forgetting and impudent,
relieved of parenting. Arenas were quite happy to comply
though a little bewildered. At first at least. One very chewy advanced
    proposition

seemed to falter, then faded into the background noise, but—here's the thing—
continued, to this day. Bald and bleeding. I don't like it, no one
is obliged to, everyone may *bon gré mal gré* ignore it, yet it peaks
and in so doing has its say. The manageress was adamant, but I had the horrible idea
of prolonging beyond night and dawn one's predilection for quoting old
dispatches and getting into hot water, and then? The sullen bathroom
question lasted, I was too far out into it, out of pocket, plus the by no means
    negligible
question of my own comfort to be decoded, and all other arguments
suddenly collapsed, like a dream of homecoming. How stung my myth;
my dream wasn't over, we were only such a dream. By this time all the caissons
of power had been turned inside out anyway; it was considered correct to despise it
and rightly so, but how often can one shamble
back to the vegetable gunk and still retain at least a superficial appearance of
    contrition?
As often as the clock seems to say I love you and boulders
turn in their sleep and sigh and the cat is forever running away. It took
two weeks to lead up to this. The stores are quiet now.
I say lie down in it. I already asked Santa about it.
And then, you see, it became part of our cultural history. We can't ignore it
even though we'd like to, it's so mild and hurtless. And you thought
you had it bad, or good. With as many associations as that
to keep thumbing through, one winks at the legal filigrane that penetrates every
page of the mouldering sheaf down to the last one, like a spike
through a door. Somebody dust these ashes off, open
the curtains, get a little light on the subject: the subject
going off on its own again. Yes but if home were only light
sliding down darkened windows in rivulets, inhabiting their
concavities and generally adapting itself to the contours of what is already there,
one could understand that,
lie back on the stiff daybed shading one's eyes from

omnipresent bleary dawn that acts as an uncle's remonstrance: do this
not for me or for yourself but for your mother the way an empty circle
of daisies seeks to promote plausibility and is simultaneously too distraught
and ashamed to articulate the siren call crisply and sinks, it too,
into the foam of reliably not taking itself seriously. I wish you well darling always
especially days when the gray pain lifts for a moment like fog trapped under
a layer of warmer air, then sags definitively not knowing what to do
with itself or about anything. Days when the pointed freshness of forests
above the snowline
can consider itself numb, when the friendly gurgling of rills talks
back and one listens but never heeds
that desire for perfectability. Hey, it was here only a moment ago
I think or somebody misled me, as sometimes happens, yet with as many
associations as that some of it is bound to come down, to crumble, to be reduced
to a vexing powder but natural like dust, and that
within all our lifetimes. Local businessmen bristled. New painless
methods were introduced but somehow made it all thick and rubbery, an
    unwanted anthem.
No one said it. Care was off and running, the divorce courts
overflowing for once, and no one was going to take issue, dispute the power vacuum
that was walking around shaking hands, acting for all the world like a candidate.
But you feel it don't you? How come nobody
has anything nice
to say, I mean you striped ball, even for a testimonial dinner on a commercial,
    then they all
run back, must have been a mistake. Yes, we have it here.

§

Anyway, where are they? I am violently opposed to the little pieces
of the puzzle getting in on the act; slobbering, as it were,
any more than I can see Little Red Riding Hood climbing Mt. McKinley.
But as for the horror of it—we are, look, all of us, undisciplined so
when it's time to take the kids somewhere or subvert the boss's ego the light
goes out of us for an instant. Oh I know we can patch it up, always successfully,
later. But out of the fine deposit of the encounter there is surely something
that is required reading, though seldom in focus. Good gravy, it
gives me the creeps just telling you about it. And after we had sunbathed
the mist was on time, dull and fathomable. That's no reason to return home, to
our roots, of course, yet neither can it be construed as an invitation. You see
everything you see on television is a fraud, is planted there to confuse distraught
patriots like yourself, and though we enter into it no wiser and leave
resolved to mend our ways, something like an actual misprint occurs. We are no
longer in charge of our propriety; jackdaws have launched nearby and the elms
        have seen
better days. Why is it that just because I'm a child I can
warn no one of this, except by speaking in tongues? Oh I know formulating
bright, snazzy, fabulous demands isn't the same thing as being a teacher
and picking up on the slowness of your student. I can rhapsodize about that
too, but there comes a point when having aimed
accurately and reaped the reasonable rewards is more than something to
sing about, is the entity, no I mean the accretion—is indeed the
fantastic fact. It was like being run over when I
first thought of this. And now sad to say our limbs
aren't as important; we have witnessed an entire tennis match and candles
are coming on, there's a hint
of fall in the air, soggy and bored. *O I have to keep fighting
back to find you, and then when you're still there, what is it I know?*
Nothing about the future and no more about you, either, honey,
I was going to say. Have you noted how things

have a way of working out but have you also noted how rarely this constitutes
    a satisfying
set of circumstances, especially when we dream, not plan, them? In my house
no one is rude but that's no excuse;
I think footfalls
are approaching, circling round, then moving away
to some other sun, some direction? I care more
yet it's there.

Despite handicaps trading continues,
natural horns bleat. The fog may be messing up traffic today
but in offices chic outfits signal that for sure violence too has its calm
aspects, when things get done in dozens, or even scores. The museum
guards must have known something was up, yet here too, only silence stammers.
Don't ask your partner what to think. He may have noticed
that the weathervane has jammed even as crowds of daytrippers
move on out of the city in gaily painted carts, and by noon something just
too awful had come between us. I called John but he couldn't come to the phone
nor did his assistant have any clue as to what the barking, the clatter
of falling jewelry were all about. It occurs to me in my home on the beach
sometimes that others must have experiences identical to mine
and are also unable to speak of them, that if we cared
enough to go into each other's psyche and explore
around, some of the canned white entrepreneurial brain food
could be reproduced in time to save the legions
of the dispossessed, and elephants. But—
what is a waiting room for, after all? If not to
live out one's life scarily to the borders of altered lawns
with red leaves nestled on them. Home becomes more than a place, more even than

a concept for this elite minority, and then singles them out
by pointing so that some symbol of their shame never
goes away, until the paper it is written on has rotted
over thousands of years, by which time new insects will have been introduced,
new forms of dandruff, holes that are really shoes. A thin puddle of air
rules over us; all obeisances are made that way, all
curtsies and notions seem to point into that vortex
of fear just as the alarm goes off. But is it
fear, or only an unpleasant hum? And jaywalkers gravitate there,
are seen to believe. The old man had no enemies. Why, then? Because a handful
of ages knew of his connection to poetry via the wet, fissured rocks far below
in the cave and took revenge for their own knowingness to create an unpleasant
situation that would probably have gone away if nobody had said anything about it,
but now—well you just can't ask people to keep silent
about something they've seen, and the forces that prodded
us on to victory are staging an uncharacteristic fast.
Only the intrusion of tomorrow's light will have been recognized as a new note
in the negotiations, which will in any case by that time be in the public
domain, and no further recruiting be deemed necessary, or undertaken.
I can't shake the hunch that this is what the stuff is all about
and no one cares to
know, let alone be a witness to further legal horse-trading.
That's what caused all the trouble.

Words, however, are not the culprit. They are at worst a placebo,
leading nowhere (though nowhere, it must be added, can sometimes be a cozy
place, preferable in many cases to somewhere), to banal if agreeable note-spinning.
Covering reams of foolscap with them won't guarantee success,

yet neither will it automatically induce ruination; wheel on the guillotine;
leave, in the middle distance, something like an endless morgue, a lake of regret.
It's better though to listen to the strange chirps of the furniture.
Listening is a patented device whose manifold uses have scarcely begun to be
      explored,
that one should practice on as many occasions as are deemed profitable. Bore
      your friends,
wine them, show them a grand time: other, more auspicious
occasions are sure to be evoked; nights when, from the grandstand, tremendous
      plumes
of steam plummeted straight into the basalt sky. Days of conversation, and,
      at the end,
a feeling of progress in sorting out mutual feelings and actually partly
resolving certain discords came to seem as though it were happening
and the treehouse was split apart by rays plunging out of the incandescent
core of tangled concerns and resolves and the handcar of an important relationship
was steered onto the right track out of the city into a shadowed, mostly empty
peripheral zone of tears for anointed and angry memories, defused now,
ready for twilight. It's something Eagle Scouts used to discuss
by the campfire, a page that somehow got ripped out of the record, to be
as though it had never been. Just because cows and horses stand around much as
      they always have,
it is as though we were contemplating a set of sealed instructions:
now the bridge will never be built,
if that is all time had in the wallet at his back. Scaled-down surprises
here and there, a puttering about in dust, and once again it seems as though it
were all up to us. Well, why not? The gravel underfoot is a little finer
this time round. And nobody yells at you. The words have, as they
always do, come full circle, dragging the meaning that was on the reverse side
all along, and one even

expects this, something to chew on. I'm rubber
and you're glue, whatever you say bounces off me and sticks to you; in which gluey
embrace I surrender. We are both part of a living thing now.

A decade later he stumbled or became confused.
There was no one else along on this outing, so why was he
always flailing his arms majestically? Talking to the walls? Whenever someone'd
cross over to be kind to him it was as though he'd never seen a human face before;
the eyes were runny, the nose ditto, the words were like chopped cotton wool
after he'd forced them out. To drag meaning like this behind one is bad
enough, but to have it beside one is worse, worse than knowing what to do.
Finally, the memory became an object
to be passed around for displays of connoisseurship to ignite; thus,
one can live in the same house with one's ambitions and
drives and still have the luxury of feeling alone: oh come off it, no
one wants to be alone. And even, you know, accept the occasional invitation
but also slog on unshod, solitary, except for casual greetings from
even more casual acquaintances.

Harder to explain is the disparity between what is loved
and the energy with which one goes about doing it, and harder still
to understand or appreciate the astonishingly thin gruel
which serves its hunger *de tous les jours* and with which
it gives every appearance of being satisfied. I suppose if one
were born and grew up on a desert island, knowing
of nothing better or even different, one might coincide
with the four walls that contain one and see no anomaly, no

grotesquerie, in the result. This mound of cold ashes that we call
for want of a better word the past wouldn't inflect the horizon
as it does here, calling attention to shapes
that resemble it and so liberating them into the bloodstream
of our collective memory: here a chicken coop, there a smokestack,
farther on an underground laboratory. These things then wouldn't
depress (or, as sometimes happens, exalt) one, and living would be just that:
a heavenly apothegm leading to a trance on earth. Yet one scolds
the horizon for having nothing better to offer. *Did I order that?*
And when the bill comes, tries to complain to the management
but at that point the jig, or whatever, is up. Yes I've seen many fine
young girls in my time take that path and wonder afterwards
what went wrong. I've seen children, taken from their homes
at too early an age, left to wander about like Little Nell,
not knowing that they were never obliged to do this thing. O
paradise, to lie in the hammock with one's book and drink,
not hearing the murmur of consternation as it moves progressively
up the decibel scale. Yet I see you are uncertain where to locate me:
here I am. And I've done more thinking about you than you perhaps realize,
yes, a sight more than you've done about *me*. Which reminds me:
when are we going to get together? I mean really—not just for a
drink and a smoke, but *really*
invade each other's privacy in a significant way that will make sense
and later amends to both of us for having done so, for I am
short of the mark despite my bluster and my swaggering,
have no real home and no one to inhabit it except you
whom I am in danger of losing permanently as a bluefish slips off
the deck of a ship, as a tuna flounders, but say, you know all that.
What kind of a chump do you think I am, anyway? I would like your
attention, not just your eyes and face. I would like to tell you
how much I love you. I'm a sap for trying, but down deep

in the bowels of the ship we hear something, don't you agree, that
tells us where we went off course and what we must do to
get back on it only now it's too late, all the
spars have erupted like apple blossoms, hitting the reef: I would
like to go on for a while anyway, but wonder under the circumstances whether
it wouldn't be like setting out on a long journey in rain so heavy
it takes your breath away. Even one step is out of the question,
I think, now. I no longer have the energy to breathe
on the windowpane so that the frost will transform it into garlands
of chiseled steel that draw one out
like a rapt interlocutrix. No it's
heavy out here today; the wind serves only to remind one of other possible
beginnings and an end, if one were likely to pass this way again.

I see.
I'll try another ticket. Meanwhile thanks for the harmonium: its
inoffensive chords swept me right off my feet near the railroad
and—nice—are returning to bloom tomorrow and each day after that.
I thought nobody needed a confessor any more, but I was wrong I guess,
so, old stump, I'm off until tomorrow or some day early next week, I mean
how much more can I say, giving myself away, without negating
the positive meaning of what I wanted to say and which has now subtly changed
back to an elementary precept or something else one doesn't much want to hear:
how we flowered, and lost, and rose up thin again with our thoughts
to distract us but not too much and so approached the shambling
roadbed and placed one sole in front of another, slowly but not tentatively,
and then the lean-to, the buttercups and the ring of blue mountains hove
into view as though to say but that's what I asked you last time
and now you will be forced to give a different answer

even though the wind has dropped. I thought I saw someone over there.
No, it's just the wind egging the trees on
into battle with dusk, and I can
still see how it's still you there, only with such a difference I almost
didn't have time to trust my space. But we know now and have had it true
to be us, for the asking, for the begging, for the just one more time.

In winter it was generally a slow blizzard of piano rags, while in summer
or some such season gentian shadows on the tapioca fields looked themselves
good enough to eat, and always in a locker downstairs was this pocket
mirror with *the* thumbprint on it, a source of shame, but how
can I deny my true origin and nature even if it's going to get me into a lot of
trouble later? At any rate, no notice was taken of anything and
maids pushed their prams and policemen stopped cars and it was getting to be spring
or it wasn't, but the bare trees looked oddly barbed, and perhaps *that*
was something, and it seemed to be starting to rain. I sit here
wringing my hands but what good does it do
if *I* am the ghost this time despite
the reassuring activity that surrounds me? And if I am to be cast off, then
where? There has to be a space, even a negative one, a slot
for me, or does there? But if all space is contained within me, then
there is no place for me to go, I am not even here, and now, and can join
no choir or club, indeed I am the sawdust of what's around but nobody can
even authorize that either. My Collected Letters will I somehow
feel vindicate me but even there the onion skin cannot be split and I'll go on
being a postscript written in invisible ink until some day several centuries from now
when they open a time capsule and enthusiastic fresh air will rush out to inform
the world and one can rise from one's nap in time for bed. The great apartment
fronts will put their heads together and sunset will seem an enormous conflagration,

but vindicate one at what price? Where are the children now who wanted
to hear that story? Why, the youngest of them passed away years ago
on the west coast surprised that anyone should remember and the slow
torrent of the glacier got piped in efficiently to fill the slightest hairline
fissure. Its job is done. We all live in the past now. And so the children
must still hang on somewhere, though no one is quite sure where or how many
or what paths there are to be taken in darkness. Only the fools, the severed
    heads, know.

So my old mother became a niche in time, and she, too, preferred not to get out of it:
as long as it was going to be, it wasn't this bad, says the antique adage. And these
three or four others came of it. No one asked them in but they came in anyway,
prepared to play. And somehow a chapter was written about this. It all
boils down to keeping quiet and having a good time. As long as you don't abuse
the orange trees standing in their pots so civil, well all will be yours next time too
and let's hear it for those who never won anything, whose time came and went
like the tide leaving curious bones behind, and they were never cheated on and never
lied, without telling anyone the truth. And behind these, interlopers
and more interlopers, a vast frame of them, too facile to be derided.
And bananas stand around stiffly, at attention. Is this
the gray way I once knew? And if so, where are the standard bearers? Why
have our values been lost? Who is going to pay for any of this?
Pottsville is too small for a man of your caliber. Full many a flower
is born to blush unseen, and waste its fragrance on the arctic air
outside the Shady Octopus saloon, and then some.

    §

If all is going to be reorganized, the charming irregularities of the days
ahead may as well go too, the song of plaintive songs choke off the ingress
while alleviating the drip, as the old man, hypotenuse-like, touches
an extremity that soon burns out of control, surrounds
the town on the down and all rush together, those who
hated each other suddenly finding good reason for the slobbering embrace.
Whether it's more fun to feel in one's own underpants
or strike out on the highroad to professional success, all pavilions a-flutter,
all portholes glinting, before the thing sinks in the mouth of the river, memory
has been transformed into corpses and while we stand discussing the news the
    unmanageable
outline of something much bigger and more profuse is struggling to understand
itself (it will be years before it gets around to us and by then
what faces will we be? Who's going to take care of the association headquarters
and, likelier still, revert with us to the narrow-gauge railroad track that steals
through yellow viburnum and buried cinders as though to point the finger of guilt
at the very beginning, the origin that is still a baby, learning to cry
as the lights are blown out and darkness like a swift film of oil closes down
to the brilliant crack at the horizon's outcome?). No two employees know it.

I thought, and this much remained hidden from me:
the beloved canker that was always there, willing to give you all of "Queen Mab"
for a quarter, or turn on the rusty heel of one boot and be off, whistling
into such nether parts of the sky as are deemed scarcely fit for consumption
here on our poor earth; the Christmas lights, each blinking in the triumph of its
individual color toward the benefit of the whole; the stars and so on brought forth
each night as a sop to the unweeded intellect, though much
more remains to be read into them; polar bears, relaxing each on his floe in the
    arctic section

of the zoo or rolling off it into the green, greasy water; people with pencils
in their hands; a selection of erotic attractions for this week including stiletto heels
and rubber miniskirts; carloads of whatever thundered past in the night; juleps
on porches; and the most extravagant collection of whodunit compliments one
was ever gifted with, out of the nightfall of a dream, freeflowing as the meanders
of a great stream, and every bit as meaningless and ominous; and finally a choice
of purgations, each not necessarily appropriate to the instance; i.e., electrocution
    for the theft
of a needle; simple tears for aggravated manslaughter; a necklace of boar's teeth
for blaspheming; added lines in the forehead for poaching, or preaching; a fountain
of mud on the front lawn of one who fondled his daughter's best friend's breasts;
and, for the discreetly ambitious, a monotonous horizon. As it all bore in
on me I started to awake, then thought better of it, then rushed to the phone to call
my broker, but it was too late: an osselet of meaning in the lizard's tail
of eternity had clicked into place, become pure and unattainable, while I, goof
that I am, simultaneously realized just how sensational it was and how a fortune
    could
be made by being first with the revelation as the bank closed its doors and the
    market suspended operations.

True, they managed to save Hitler's brain before it destroyed the world
with *zuppa inglese*. (Just look in the milk can and you'll find out why.) But
    sometimes
walking away from a cure may not be the best way to get rid of it. Sure, you feel
fine. Today, and tomorrow as well. By next week you're feeling better
than you have in a long time. And as the medication gradually dissipates, the
    feeling of
well-being takes over, an arbiter for generations to come. Only long after your death

will the life you so busily led be imputed to the cornerstone of rot that was
the secret, driving force in it: something everyone at the time found to be OK.
And as gravel sinks slowly with the aquifer's depletion, those
not in the know will begin to stir in their sleep; it will gradually dawn on them
(in dreams of "cheese, toasted mostly") how the ingenious theory was flawed; indeed
it was flaws that produced the dazzling quicksilver sheen that attracted
so many to it for so long. If that's the case, why tarry on rutted goat-paths
from whence even the nearest foothills are shrouded, by mists, from view? The
    animals
are incredible; there's even a dog named Bruce. One can retool the context, but
    slowly,
slowly, and of course there is no positive guarantee of a successful outcome; one
should think of it as a virtuoso spinning-song whose relentless *roulades* promise
    minor
disturbances among the cobwebbed rafters but perhaps nothing much to weave
one-armed nightshirts with for the wild swans, your brothers: only
try to forget the slow upward
path to perfectness and let its mirror-image
come to install its truly sensitive surface within you, during the night
of deft dreams and bad brushes with dolor. Fear of the dark causes it,
but by then to have been around and been of it will have carried over into lunch.
Do you think there's some connection between this and that which happened
    before?
Perhaps not. Perhaps there is none, but the Patagonians will like it, all 499,500 of 'em.

Without further ado bring on the subject of these
negotiations. They all would like to collect it always, but since
that's impossible, the Logos alone will have to suffice.

A pity, since no one has seen it recently. Others crowded the opening, hoping
to catch a glimpse, but the majority saw the occluded expatriate ragtag
        representation and
decided to not even try. To this day no one knows the shape or heft of the thing,
and that's the honest truth thrown out of court, exhibiting abrasions,
muffled. And the story of how we ran out of it.

So, "marrying little with less," *meliora probant, deteriora*
sequuntur, they footdrag in oblivion, lingering over steaks to analyze
the latest inquiry.

My biological father thought enough of it to see that I was posited, demanding
names omitted from the roster, either from carelessness or intent to harm: *we'll*
see that the thing gets done! And moreover, as I was asking her about her car
a quiet moment of fatigue slipped in leaving faces drained, moments of pleasure
unexamined. It was all because I told him he should change his shirt. He got mad
and went out and I didn't see him again for thirty years, by which time both of
        us had aged
considerably but were still reasonably attractive, some might even say more so. I
reminded him of the shirt thing and he just laughed, said supermarkets sell
        them now
and besides you shouldn't worry about a little dirt, it's the spice of life, he said.
And we had set aside Siberia
for us and for a few beloved friends
but the bureaucracy and the logistics of it all defeated us, why we were tied
up in red tape for 2½ years and after that I just wanted out, no

place is worth that much worry. Besides it's quite quiet and confusing at home,
    thank you
very much. Yet I was still hung up on his idea of me, I thought I was becoming
    that person
I didn't even know or want to know very much about, and all of my
déjà-vus were ones that could have occurred to him. Still, life is reasonably absorbing
and there's a lot of nice people around. Most days are well fed
and relaxing, and one can improve one's mind a little
by going out to a film or having a chat with that special friend; and before
you know it it's time to brush your teeth and go to bed. Why then, does that feeling
of emptiness keep turning up like a stranger you've seen dozens of times, out-of-focus
usually, standing toward the rear of the bus or fishing for coins at the newsstand? I'm
sure it's all coincidence, but it
does have a way of rattling things, like a constant draft through the house, rustling
papers, riveting one's eye on the clock. So what's
to feel nervous about? We all know that we have to live for a certain time and then
unfortunately we must die, and after that no one is sure what happens. Accounts
    vary. But we
most of us feel we'll be made comfortable for much of the time after that, and
    get credit
for the (admittedly) few nice things we did, and no one is going to make too much
of a fuss over those we'd rather draw the curtain over, and besides, we can't see
much that was wrong in them, there are two sides to every question. Yet the facts
fascinate one, we become one of those persons who are only satisfied with thoroughly
reliable information—the truth, if there ever could be such a thing. Our journey
flows past us like ice chunks, maybe it is we that are stationary.
O so much God to police everything and still be left over to flatter one's
harmless idiosyncrasies, the things that make us *us*, which is precisely
what is fading like paint on a sign, no matter how much one pretends it's the same
as yesterday. And children talk to us—*that*, surely, must be a plus?

§

It's the lunatic frequency this time. One man, taking his kids to the ball
game, reverted and was found playing cards at a friend's house. In spring the tips of
the apple branches graze the trailer and it's time for a new round
robin of progressive delicacies and returned thank-you letters. Out in the open
by the gym it was never a question of keep your pants on we're all getting
    someplace, getting
to be someone. Those were perspectives too limned to shoot along and the
    people thanked
the baseball player who invented them. Inactivity is as a syrup to these people,
    some of them,
they bank on mistrust and in the end are amazed to find their land has been
    overgrazed
by herds of yak, each of the quadrupeds spaced almost equidistant from its
nearest neighbor, as far as the eye can see, to Labrador and beyond
into the topaz twilight of the Urals. Oh some will say
you can't trust them let alone see them coming, let alone avoid a collision
with jarring implications for the future of humanity. Even its garish exterior
isn't as uncompromising as one might
at first conclude, and then they have ashtrays and can see, no one makes
    extraordinary
demands on them as long as they go on living, and in April
that doesn't seem an impossible feat. To those residing on the outskirts of some
city or suburb it gets to be even more of a tease—were *they* included in the
    survey, and,
if so, who are they? Shooting-gallery ducks waiting to be flattened, probably.
What if one crosses the sea
to descend at the pier where one's sweetheart bade farewell to one several years
    ago and finds

her there to greet one, not all that changed? And if the parents of both parties
      pronounce it
a suitable match, why there you are, another union has been consecrated, another
two people been driven from loneliness into the reciprocal dawn of each other's arms
as if it were long ago, and tidings spread throughout the land and ordinary people
came to appreciate and savor and go back into the narrow, closetlike conundrum
      of their own
slender existences and be thankful there was for once something to talk about and then
mutually agree on. A pact with the forces that be—nothing less, and that
is saying a good deal. So in all eras bargains have been struck,
horns blown, and in some strange, silly way each of us is the stronger for it. We made
our tea and then we drank it. This is an honorable instance of how shame can
      disappear
in the dust and the confusion, the aftermath. And if an executive
can teeter on his perch all day long from dawn to dusk, a wren
can say to him, why don't you go on an organized outing, stop
fooling yourself, this world-situation isn't nonsense though *realpolitik* may not be
the accurate term for it either, so why explode like a timebomb that was set long ago
and may no longer be operable? But you see so many
of us are like that bird, that man I mean, that for but a few can life resonate with
anything like serious implications. So many were hung out to dry, or, more
      accurately, to rot.
And these marginalia—what other word is there for them?—are the substance
      of the text,
by not being allowed to fit in. One can proceed like a ghost
along corridors and find that doors are closed to one, and then
what good is being invisible? It all goes to show how our parents taught us
      many things,
including the right one, that we should untie
gently, like a knotted shoelace, and then little expressions of relief occur in the
      whorls,

and many things, incipient ones, besides. Yet on the shoals of this time
everyone believes himself righteous and lost, that the view is only a way
in all directions, and one must have a timepiece to unravel ramifications that
in fact do not exist, but like a gold toothpick are merely on hand to see that they
get talked about and maybe some club will invite one of them to speak. It is an air
strangely purged of magnolias, and quicklime, and anyone
can be called to take a seat. Best to enjoy it,
not turn up in the unwritten part as a miser or scavenger few would have taken
    seriously
as a person, but just as many might have feared. We live in an age when terror
opens like breadfruit and one *must* pick and choose—the seeds and proverbs just
aren't that numerous. Everybody must vote. Everybody's vote must be accepted
    into the
tilting radio tower that is collapsing in one's own best interest in one
dark swoop of mingled horror and relaxed apprehension: to accomplish
anything more would be a joke, yet
the boy
still stands there, hasn't gone away; by any
other standards a misadventure yet one is going to be firm and tame and positive
in searching out the old prescription, scratching one's
first initial idly in the wood of the door and only then
going away, to be something else in some other town when newspapers bearing
that day's date finally arrive and the citizenry, perplexed, still goes about its business
carrying news of new situations into inaccessible corners of this bland
and stultified universe, only to be someone
isn't then their top priority: getting to be tall in late afternoon is.
The arrogance of these people! Anyone who's been around understands, and that
includes most of us: barristers . . . Out of one's loneliness it's hard not to forgive
the girl who longs to be seen, and the guy who wishes only to be left alone. Forest
dithers protect us a lot of the time, but for those moments when one is thrust willy-
nilly into the spotlight, then oh dear! I wish I had something more sizable to say—

couldn't my part be rewritten? But that's over too before long. And the forest
    comes to
seem more like a commodity, somewhere one can live and tie rope around oneself.
The annals, if there are any, transform this into glamour and chrysoprase, two
adjacent keys of a piano pressed down one after the other. And one's modesty—
well it's all here, in this manila folder. I was going to talk about that, tree
of the deep, tree of being beautiful of, of lost promise and hopes
that still flutter in the distance, and you know somehow . . . But in the end it
    got mistreated,
the happy moments streaked with sadness, but perhaps they always were.
Perhaps it says a great deal that there were any, and so
out of tune with the rest that was going on, like a canary in a zoo, and I said
why give any guarantees if it can be rescinded without notice, if entreaties are to
become comments, and you know what he said, he said, well, it's reasonable for
    you to expect that
but it's not unreasonable for anyone else to pay it no mind, so there! I was
crushed. The one person I thought understood. But it's all right, he can go on paying,
meanwhile I am scarcely alone, though it *is* lonesome. However, when I start
feeling blue I can just stand up like everyone else and lay my cards on the table: look,
it says so, it's all here, written in this book. So I'm never completely at a loss,
only a little disconcerted, thrashing about, sometimes. In the rival cesspool
of other nations they may think they have it better, but I know that here the
uncertainty is pure. And so I often take the afternoon off, read, write or gaze
intently out of the window for long periods of time. And then you take tea
in the afternoon, that is you make it and then drink it. Oh I'm so sorry, golly, how
nothing ever really comes to fruition. But by the same token I am relieved of
    manifold responsibilities,
am allowed to delegate authority, and before I know it, my mood
has changed, like a torn circus poster that becomes pristine again in reverse
    cinematography,
and these moments of course matter, and fall by the wayside in a positive sense.

Perplexed by myopia one still enjoys it, and in the autumn of life cackles
    somewhat unrestrainedly
before writing off one's accurate perception
of all that has gone before in the heroic period when books are friends. Nature
wants you to do it. No seism infinitesimal enough not to register in the growing
tornado of disapproval when mountains crash in the rubble, electricity bisects
    the sky, and
shrill ululations burst forth from caverns deep in the earth's surface. But I'm
getting ahead of my story, we're talking about how you, a wanderer, like it,
and how to escape. Oh my dear, I've tried that. But if it interests you
you can browse through this catalog and, who knows, perhaps come up with a
    solution that will apply
to your complicated case, just conceivably, or perhaps you know someone better
    informed
in the higher echelons where the view is distant and severe,
the ground blue as steel.

II

But how trivial the music. All this. Yet it is where part of the gender first starts to
emerge and become a blur. The various members
of both sexes never seem to get hurt: theirs is a life that drifts peaceably along
as on a stream and they can wave
to each other like boats and join in the fun and never be forgotten. Possibly
a door opens far down in the wall to admit a lover
who as silently departs later. Possibly there is more to it all than this,
but if we can decipher even what the fair-minded man wants us to, what about the rest,
poverty and disclaimers? And who sees the mountain-mad man through goatshine
and never confesses to an early blunder concealed, to having left a child in the
        cold once?
And as they marginally edge each other, new and good truths and others, older
and not so good, begin to appear along the bicycle-trail of their itinerary
through space, here on earth. One was a Spanish longshoreman's daughter,
a laughing girl, who, when told the truth, deliberately spat on it. Another,
young too, and in the full flower of "the devil's beauty," had good cause to come
        up and grab
an arm, an elbow resting on a newspaper as it happened, and tickle the thing
half to death. And in the interval of slide, or portamento, a lot of laughing does
get to be heard, only it's like you're not doing it, it's the boys
on the other side of the ridge obeying their zeal again. The moon abruptly
        decides to set

and kids pester their parents for more firecrackers, in the crevices, where eyes
lately peeked out—O bored hero,
why not return to earth for a while? We have forgiven thee
what was construed as negligence rather than rancor, so in return we
should be taught by thy knee. Later when she comes to throw out the table
        scraps there it will be,
a little sliver of haven made and purposely rigged for you
to come and go many times without noticing, slinging your coat over your shoulder
as you go along looking in the dirt for a whistle. But that day
it was all roses. And it turned out that the inquiry was silenced,
deliberately erased from the file.
And if a man wanted this, and got it, how about the heathen rest of us
who wait in silence for food
as though a drug got planted in one's abdomen? Sooner or later, boys and girls
        declare, there
will be someone on whom a care like this could devolve,
a woman made to see through, analyze, and correct the errant circuitry
and in doing so bring us back to the harbor of recollection
from which we strayed so long ago, but it was a mistake in a dream.
The formula is now reconstituted.
From the awfulness of times long gone by it wrests
a polite excuse, small even by its standards, but alive to us, and harsh, dry, a
        wrong prism.

Or stand: all right, lowering the teabag into the mug until something
comes of it, is plumbed, but meanwhile what of zombies standing around in
        clinging seersucker
in frigid temperatures, awaiting your decision? When the curse
arrives, are you prepared to deal with it? Apologies don't matter any more; it's

a question of biting off the end, spitting it out, and sucking the poison through a
    small tube
if you want to go that way. Otherwise, listless years of atrophy could be your fate
though there are undoubtedly worse ones. Pick a channel, explore, document it—
please take *all* the evidence into account in your report, when you write it:
you'll find your story isn't so different from any honest man's, nor less
bizarre and compelling: was it always a savage rite? Weren't there times
in childhood when one felt neutral, a shy appraiser gazing unendangered into
the reflecting globe, and when you turned back, moments later, the horrible clashes
hadn't gone away, but you were somehow separated, a person with things to do?
    And if
the urgency thinned out in later decades, why be compromised? Because these others
were waging war on things and people with words and things does it follow
    that your employment
was slighted, that you weren't free to clean out your desk? Sullen
newsprint blows back and forth, a double sheet of it is suddenly tossed six stories high
and drops back, heavy as a sinker: does this have something
to do to you; more to the point, are you alive severed from it? The old ghouls
will have to be derided before one faces up to the specter of the empty stadium
at dusk, bare branches aquiver. How about your friend
in the hospital: did you call him? How many bridges between here and the
    end of that journey?
Over wells, along walls, silently one creeps along. Employment is difficult: I mean
it's difficult for me to hold a job long, not that I'm not efficient, it's, well,
so easy not to understand, to take full possession of one's unawareness and
then refuse to leave, a squatter in one's own house. And so much will
have happened by the time even this minor wrangle is settled. It's impossible
to keep abreast of the times, and yet we still think of wings.

§

How soft were those mute,
eloquent colors; even the plaids were like subtle hints. One baked
under trees, too lazy to notice the fading hour, until
the alarm sounded, the park went berserk, and then? Meanwhile a decision
    about keeping and
refinancing the old records had been reached, sure enough, just as one arrived
    home out
of breath. They said no one will ever speak to you now. Because in the dark
you knew something and didn't tell it, though the darkened spaces under the
    trees were at that
point intolerable, their bulk like mere hulls in the shattered night light. Better
to go into exile early rather than late, you thought, not saying anything, but the
    notion
became a battle-cry and soon everybody was trying to disconnect his life and seal it
off, unsuccessfully. The idea had occurred to you during a performance of a
    high-school play.
You weren't ashamed to take credit for it—why should you be? And thus a field
got sorted out; all the husks, shadows and little bells counted and clear in the rising
tide of shadow that steeped and proclaimed it: here was another place
to take orders in, to be from if convenient; only don't die
yet, we'll need you for the next act; it suited everybody.

Not on the agenda was the piercing squeal of puffins
newly released from captivity—but we'd get to that, later. Now the news
was of inflation. How to combat it? Is there any world-power so stupid it thinks it
must have the answer, or that an answer actually exists? You can bet there isn't,
which isn't a reason for a lot of ink and newsprint not to get chewed up in the approach
to an argument on the subject. Those peaceful voices, rising tier on tier

in the storied gothic cathedral, go unheard. Nobody thinks it's time for them,
and so, when one has become a little more exhausted, one
sinks down with one's lunch under a lofty elm in the breathless, shrunken noon.
Did one perhaps oversell oneself,
and if so how many instances are left? Miss Winslow was just telling us about
    your island
and its cormorants and the—er—other problems. How do the natives feel
about what you're doing? Is there any way to escape butchery
before it's too late, except in the exploding haystacks? But I get ahead of myself—I'll
do anything—that is, anything I can—to avoid the appearance of inequity, only
    please,
please call those spear-carriers or whatever you call them off.
Once two were saddled with each other's lies which became as a sacramental trust
for them. They listened, they put forth feelers, pouted on cue, but in due
course banshees exploited the situation. And once the climate of trust is destroyed
only lust for vengeance can take its place—or so *one* would have us believe.
After school I told some of the parents about it. On this site
exactly ten years ago stood an oblong wooden toll booth. Now there's not
a trace to indicate anything ever existed here. Kind of makes you wonder how
this place will look when you're gone. Oh you needn't throw bones
at it, the attendants are churlish enough—still, I've got to see one of those
so-called ant men before I leave here, which better be quick. But don't drag us
back to the water hole, I can see my reflection just fine in this bent
piece of aluminum. My hair, today, is beautifully combed. I am on a roll, I
    guess, and two
medicine men are coming to tea, and their letters of recommendation have
    already been mailed,
and so for two years out of vanity I shifted my position on the stool, pretending
    indifference
to everything, though I knew, in my heart of hearts, this wasn't the way

to gain their trust, or mine. And now that it's time to give out prizes, why
there just isn't any gumption left, only wheezes, so we all must stay and then go
away unsatisfied. It was no good grumbling about the weather;
it always came just the same, and left us
feeling vaguely unsatisfied.
A proud pair they were: unscathed for a day.
Interestingly, he hadn't done all the things he said he had.
Which doesn't solve the problem of white-glove inspections and seeds that roll
after they have been planted. Should he have been feeling more anxiety? Nah.
    Generating
trust? Depends on whose. Any one of several roadblocks could have deterred
    whatever
was escaping, and she (in green dress) was doing a masterful job of distracting
    the parking-
lot attendant. On the morning of the following day we found ourselves
    confronted with the
familiar problem of too much desert and too little time. Friends—you know the
    feeling—
are going to insist on knowing whose story it is. Better tell them. But wait—
you can't relate something and then connect it to some specific person. No job
says you ought to. But, heavy with garlands, we were being followed by the police
into a set-up storefront. Here, it all ends. Not so fast—we may have other
    information
to absolve wage-earners of paying dues
to your rotten club with all its intimate signs and shivers
of remorseless joy. Thought you had me. You'll face the Luftwaffe—alone.
    Now there's
a young woman outside says she has some important information about Mrs.
    Butterfield.
Young lady, is this a trick? What about the spiders that drilled all day, maneuvers

that took up so much time the judge never got around to depositing the check
     and the
bingo night went kerflooey, what with the sounds of drenching rain, leaks in
     the shutters,
pivotal oilcloth sentiments peeling, junked party ornaments, a woman who says
     he's a size 11
and other gadabouts, listless ones, too revealing to report on? The chimney
     seemed about to collapse,
disguising the fact that a mountain of sludge was moving on
the hysterical town, all of whose gaily decorated ridgepoles were in danger, only
     now no one
stopped to think about it, the more massive southwestern face being turned
     toward one
and all, who, mesmerized by the silence of death, made sure their seams
were straight. It seemed but a few moments later though actually it was
     probably more like
years that the evangelist profited and whispered: all of his
town made sense, his relatives enjoyed positions of respect, and so
what trouble could there be? No, there is no knocking in the walls, nothing
like that. The operation is a success from the point of view of the furthest tangle
of violet cliff-face that sometimes flashes toward one, far across the valley, as though
     revealing
an ecstatic, deep-buried message. This is the price we have to pay,
it seems to say, and though all future debts will have been incurred gladly, one must
shoulder the burden of the interest payments NOW, otherwise there'll be such a
     scare
in the curriculum as only the oldest ones will want to get out, the others
impeded or impeached by the books they have a right to read
in this our own time. Only I say to you, don't look askance at the singers
just because they're not responsible for the awful libretto, bearing in mind the tropes

each had to traverse to get here, and now their music delights the eye
and the mind as well as the ear, they have surely calibrated their longings to us;
there will be more surprises to come and the well-nursed fantasy expands, blooms
with the hair of their yearning, turning desire to a trick and love to its own
    advantage.
Yet come speak with me behind the screen of the waterfall's Holophane, yet be
    not too
distant lest the muggers suspect us and the children bear away our burden, our only
secret. For nurseries have their news agencies as surely as garlic repels vampires
among others. Today a tree talked to us. What it said was don't
plunge too deeply into the microbe-infested waters, there may be an alternate plan
which will allow us to save more lives and so become our own resurrection of sorts
on the simple chart. Pin it here, it says, this place is the most valuable and least
congested with shit and other rungs of the ladder of hysterical flight
from the pages of a magazine to the dime-store trophy that is your secret,
    haunted
by memories both reluctant and relaxed, as long as it wants to take you away.
    But beware
the instant in which it doesn't: utopias can crumble
in that split-second, and you may wake up finding you have more than you ever
    wanted to own,
but by that time the dream is falling in on itself in slow motion or someone is
    dismantling it.

Here at Shadowlawn the question is always: O what awful thing are they doing
    now?
What make-believe? Idiotic proposals are advanced, then they blab it,
it won't work. It doesn't work. Not that anyone is what I would call conceited, or

outgoing either, I guess. There's a certain image . . . But that went out in 1971.
   No one has
been back there since. A small road leads to it, called "the esplanade." In small
   groups
they recur, since the fence was last painted, and are up to discussing it—who knows,
maybe an interesting idea will emerge, yet the handwriting on the wall seems to
   indicate otherwise:
return to your abstractions, it said, life
has no need of you just yet. I was sitting in my car
and suddenly I could see down the whole distance I had come, and the fog-
   shrouded destination
became clear again, as it has so many times over the past weeks. I thought I should
sharpen my appearance, for that way lies light, lies life, and yes I am
talking about new clothes as well. He wore a black suit—
that's what image those threads project? Arts & leisure—80 bucks! As quiet as my
contentment is the voice at my shoulder: make it over. Perhaps not a total
from-the-ground-up rehab, perhaps only a few cosmetic touches
would have an earth-shaking impact, in this instance. It's what you *can* do that
   matters
more than the whole picture, but the older we grow, the more unused to the
   idea of dying—
and I'm sorry I brought the subject up—we become. We are set in our ways. The
   breath
of autumn is vast again, we see vague but kind-hearted auguries
in it, then forget. It's the way our silhouette gets projected on invisible nature
that seduces one to come down from the top of the leaf-pile. By then it's dark,
of course. One's sedan's not on schedule, and the rear-view mirror is brittle, too
polished to shine, just visible enough to see the hairs
on one's face by. Is it going to cripple
our image of our self-esteem? Where were we in the dark? Can you see it? Positive?

§

Not so nice now, as the deep cranberry-colored berries linger
on the trees though shriveled and cold—surely not till summer? But that's
ages away and I have to finish my story, and character
is what I forgot to add. O but it will change
the negative nature of it, put in something we don't need all right,
gigantic though it be. Still, and though the leaves are only threaded on the
    branches now,
someone has to look after it. I never had a servant. Always, I was accustomed
to doing my own cleaning, even as others were not. Heck, what creeps
are these? And I forgot the way back, forgot the back of the story,
perhaps for the better, since I was refreshed and could remember nothing,
nothing of what happened so long ago, on a certain evening
in July. We called across
shallow lagoons to each other; it seemed to help. Now to expunge
the revenge-motif, and get it all right for once. Life is an embroidery-frame, and
    what you put
into it gets left there, there are so many kinds of designs, literally millions of them
and the combinations of these—well. So perhaps what happened at Nuremberg
    in 1658 is
of some importance to me, but surely
the burden of proof doesn't rest on you. It's all I can do
for you baby now that I have to get going, but think
of the diminishing tiers of clouds clustered to the ever-more-distant horizon: do
    you want
our heritage? Or should you invest in something? And as one tendril
after another unclasps, what more is there to say? I can see you
in the ski-picture, as dazed and clean as in the old days behind the laundry,
and yet each word of what we said to each other matters, pulls, I don't know, away

like a sheet from the substance, and what are you going to get after that?
What me, huh?

I wish I could hear birdsong in those old days,
you know, the kind there used to be. It seemed every thorn was alight.
Here there is nowhere near the expansive atmosphere
we imagine we miss. Only a sullen waiter
in a soiled white jacket who slams down the coffee cups in front of you and then
    walks away.
I was told about it on a Sunday. By Monday the dogs were back, fighting over
    some used
excrement, half in the water. Wow. What a dumb thing. Only I hear he used to
    go behind
the other building, and no one knew him. But he can't say for sure. It's like a
    chicken.
I'm sure Babs remembers the time of the arguments we used to go through.
That's ancient history now, though. And, like history, it has a definite interest,
like Thebes. Curiously I was just talking
about it professor, to get it not quite wrong again, and you came up and asked me
how my theorem was and I blurted out the truth. It's all okay. It's not going to
    be divided,
not divided up among several participants anyway.

It was decided to proceed another way
while I was out of the room.
The startling freshness of it blinkered me
opposing me to many angles of lights

that fell before the door frame. A weathered quince
asked to be included. Round shrubs duly unwrapped
after winter and how do you get hold of these? Sipping a glass of brandy
my mother high above the city shooed
inset chimes to their places; how far
and how many balloons see the light of morning each time this year
and one must have a peg to hang it on, and something to walk upon,
yet it got no worse,
the time between the horse's lazily but abruptly twitched tail to
the flies from off the stable:
fellows who hurry by you,
they are taking you, out of the catalog, to
obnoxious rendezvous. Meetings. Was it ever a catbird that called thus,
got us late after school, how much we were loving it, instant
in each other's arms, and one thin one called down, that was a wave of air
to take the place away. And you and I, in our sun-kit,
we must have mastered many foreign dances,
been seen tall at the fair, for one or more of them to recognize us outside
the precinct, and to have got off scot-free for a wad
of cloth, roll of hair brushed from the comb, that's
all we were meant to see. But in the dark you see more,
especially if you're a child, and know instinctively what goes on there,
how matchbooks are bent open backwards, what warts they all
came to learn, in thin haze
out over San Francisco. I said you are my teacher Herr Schmidt,
I am the toad and pupil, you are after all all
you set out to be and it's true isn't it? It's come true, look? And his puppy-eyes
appraised mine, I was won over instantly, from that day
never thought forward, looked backward, rain
or shine, from that anointed moment
I first kissed a king in you. What reflections!

We are lucky to have this
yet one doesn't want to go, makes
excuses not to, toe twisting in door-jamb.
You flattered me I was higher up on the ladder
than any of the other pupils, and when I came to be eight, straight
as two twigs in the barn after love,
the waters receded and left.
Now's the time. But my fatal shyness overcame me
once again. I hurried out, threw
myself down the street. You see I wasn't going to be a good boy.
They just came. Took me. Now I angle pleasantly
toward the surface, thinking a good, fat dream: oh to be stuck
in there again. But the fire-engine
won't let me, the banging hurtling toward a concussion
on rocks, a broken pedestal and here,
here we stand, the breeze is pleasant so let's take
our time and sing one more song, eyes rolling,
and roam at will, timeless:

indeed I have no doubt it can be so.
Oh I don't know, do you?
What is it makes the window-maker go off on his own, if not
this sacred season of lips,
gray moisture that squeezes down on us so hard. And we are never
on our own. Because someone decreed we were not to be. And in glacial
pockets of this repercussion were still not meant to be ourselves, until
some cruel stranger forces us to be, and leaves. Ah, but then, what new
problems, taxis, taking years to get an accounting, while daffodils, long dead,
    continue

to droop sideways. Meanwhile the same film strip
is projected endlessly across one's forehead. One has seen it so many times!
Yet one dares to admit there are details, each time, that escaped one before,
like the title on the spine of the book laying on the table: The Taming of the
      Shrew. Once
mastered all this can still instruct far into the pale vacuum
one wants so much to come to know. It is strangely familiar, like a woodcutter
eating bread *dans un bois solitaire*: O my friends and sisters, haven't you
ever taken the position that what knows, grows? And familiar noodles are served.
One wants, not to like, but to live in, the structure of things, and this is
the first great mistake, from which all the others, down to the tiniest
speck, bead of snot on a child's nose, proceed in brisk military fashion, encouraging
to some on a chilly afternoon in March. What they have to say about you never
      recurs;
the fräulein, in the nadir of a pause, takes up some other subject. It's jewels.
Or a foray into the unexplained outside. We can never have tears enough,
in fact, so why regret the sun's pointing
these acerated surfaces? Once, a whale will be kind, and no other grief can exist after
that. You just have to choose, making sure all the choices are wrong, and the sky then
of your own privacy caves in on you, collapses, is comfortable as sleep. In that distant
forest nothing can live separate, and it's a dream. A difficulty. For one.
For one exchanging one neutral memory for another.

And one fans out over the abyss. This is spring, the warning:
herring may never happen again, and if one gray suit bulges before your eyes be sure
to take it in again: others may be found wanting, the gold rush having resumed,
      and operas
are once again in demand. By the time I got to the movies it was incredibly
quiet in the dark, only birds peeped, the silent man turned, and the chrome angle

of one's glasses inaccurately suggested the thirties to legions half-ignorant of
    their own
birthplaces, let alone metal screening. One has done so much for others; must it be?
No hint of lavender, of cirrus, of citrus? No but the lemmings trot back, you
    can see for yourself
how much potential was invested there, and what came of it.
It's time to swing out on one's own and, if perennial pathos isn't your dish,
make a stew of something else—nimbus, or limbo. Anything so long as it's not
    caused by neighbors
whose potential for wrecking your life is greater now than at any point in the future
provided you let them get away with it and are not angry to relinquish
the paws that go on escaping. Talk it over with your gardener, see
the bright shoots, forget that you will live long, that all thrives, apace and at the
    same rate.
Or bright facets could interrupt, reflectors
left out on lawns not live to see the dawning of new, earthen flowers
and yet be called to resume again, for dull
is not dull enough and we wish these stones to have duration even as fatigue palls
on the island in the sunset,
and flamingos fall over each other in the luxury of getting away.

I would assemble
landscapes from insect-tunneled wood and go live in a hole somewhere
lest pleasant anomalies impose bumptious charades promoting peace to others
    and to all comers,
seal it in a chest, rip it open, scatter the powder of life on the dead sawdust
to watch it blink, and then pound with my fists as hard as I can on the saga of
the sheepgirl and her friend the pelican merchant: how they became friends
    long after

ceasing to know each other, when both were blind and living in unfatally dingy
circumstances somewhere near Clapham Common: when autumn flickers,
        curves in
on the unfinished lunch, may it rest established early. To graduate
from sultry "other woman" parts to hell itself, which is infinitely more far-reaching
and beautiful than you might ever imagine, isn't the first step,
but something more like the emerging at the top of the monument, that lets you see
in the vastest if not the least clotted vistas and places
no value-judgment on your being there, on the fact of your being there, though
it might if you weren't alone, innocent
as a lintel. Back into the past, they sob, the others; it's necessary in order to
flush out the present as it were, yet one can't envy them the pained, coming-
        apart-in-high-velocity-winds feeling
or be surprised that one's reassurances are ignored. That would belong to an earlier
grand idea of the importance of one's actions, while now
almost any input is suspect, even the most cost-efficient, so that it seems other men's
gardens get all the moisture and sunlight. We on the other hand have
only sterile notions of staying included to ruffle through, and one never tires
of this retrograde motion, even as one fears the consequences of standing still
and becoming like an old chromo on a wall.
                            And yet, dozens
of others experience it, no stigma is attached, only rolling over and over like a marble
that can never stop rolling and here we are, still doing it only advised of our
        interlocutor's
growing lack of patience, and permanently eager for the end of the run,
dog bite dog, it doesn't so much say it on the advertisement as
what do you think, where do you come from; more doses of advice
from shaggy-haired strangers.
                            And all lock themselves in at night,
desperately vamping where a half-turn to see who's behind in that tree might

have been deemed more appropriate, if equally ineffective. What brio in your
    chat, how
do you keep going next time?
                                And I told him for half a dime I'd quit and screw
you too, only that's not done, the very
pillars of our civilization would crumble and Osiris would again have to punish
the unwary who danced jigs in our shadow, we the keepers of the trust who have to
somehow find the missing key that at this moment is within the grasp of a leper
who plays with it, not knowing.

And flies still tax us with their lessons: when will we give up? In order to land
    on that shred
of inhospitable strand one is forced to jettison certain
much-beloved possessions, including, I'm afraid, that key. O if only one
    belonged to something,
life would be harder perhaps but we'd have the strength to go along with
    whatever they
wanted us to say and we'd have rivalry at the end, sure, but cunning as well in
    the abstract
clockface of accusations from the various points of the compass, and who
    knows, if one got
away, how much sicker the other would get? Perhaps not much. Perhaps if you had
a little compassion in your yard things would grow staler and the calm
of the original compact wouldn't capsize it, leading to distant benefits and premises.
I told you his name was Max you were the one who thought otherwise and well
it's just as well as the gunwale unkisses faster the tires nailed to the dock
of departure and all our plans and ammo were scuttled, at the threshold
of this adamantine resort where two

can lie but no more, reprisals splash into the night. It must surely have come
from over there, those dried grasses. More power to them, for what must never
seem to have taken place on an afternoon once. As we kindle interest in that old
       past, what
astonishing trills one hears, what blistering swamp flowers thrust open; furry
sea-creatures invade the royal compound and next week the clock will strike
exactly at twelve o'clock, you'll be free of a long-tendered obligation.
Since then I've been sleeping better too, but your shoes aren't getting fed
       properly, there are
spots on whatever one is called to drink, and curse it, no
water in the watering-trough. Yes but the horse said he didn't want any, besides
his harness is torn and angry,
a proverb for the industrious. Oh we've known a long time how much her
trail was costing her and others and now it's time for definitive common
       knowledge, only
nothing is so sure anymore it wants to be reminded. Maybe it never knew at all.
       Maybe
we deduced it out of guilt, and now it's we on the run, my goodness how the
       unrolling
scenery veers past. Was it even we
who were meant to start on this race? Might it have been for the others, all for them,
and so one is let off lightly, or so it seems, with a reprimand
and a startling dream? I told someone at the start of this
I wouldn't play faster than my nearest neighbor. Now look
what's become of him. I wouldn't want to end up at a finish line unwashed
and looking like that. I go. I come later. You all land at the bottom of a
       crowded funnel
and so whatever joke is cracked coincides with your defense. Not everyone was
       made to wear
what we choose to wear. The colors, rinsed, insistent, return; the pink is for you,
not just to wash and wish desperately into something else that in any case

was probably never meant to be understood, and it smiles, and salvages
what little it can from the eternal barren beginning of March. Just two;
the alibi would only cover two; it's over; we are lost
in the habit, smiling in a foxglove tent; but the doves requested permission to
    weave over us
like psalms and sometimes the sun is good, but it just seems like it won't go away
the way a song does, leaving a slightly hollowed path behind. We could follow,
but the brimming lake on the horizon is more likely to join us if we
don't absolve ourselves, recklessly dreaming. In time all excuses merge in an arch
whose keystone overlooks heaven, and
we must be patient if we are to live that far, at our own expense, this time,
    without that.

Bet there was some falling off there; still, amid the hoo-ha concerning new
    appointments and
such there was no time to discern; new people there, android sleep rains down
on pinched neighbors like ingots of silver, and there's no mess, only a poking
    among reeds.
The last recognizable mentor left; it was up to the remains of his flock to
    reconstitute,
but left to their own devices many fled the comparative safety of the coop for used-
car lots, car washes, drive-in banks, in order so to speak to get their heads together.
I was the only one of my squadron to count them as they left in single file,
but not being able to do much about it, or keep records, soon I too was lost—
    well, not exactly,
but tethered expectations always result when you go a little too far in one
    direction, not
enough in another, and betimes one spots the calendar on the office wall: think, it says.
Like a plangent river my life has unrolled this far, to a fraction of this place,

and I have commandeered motor launches, but it has all been in vain, this
     celebration: listen,
what do children think of you now? Suddenly everyone is younger, and many
     of them not all
that young, either, and who, do you suppose, loves you? It's a variant of the
     shell game
again; not all its premises are suicidal, but where is the one who takes out the ashes,
leaves the key behind? Up through the frantic town he rages ("It works, it's bent
but it works!") like the wing of a plane but we always knew it was here, sure
     we did, Ma I'll tell you later
in the meantime and lilac bushes are a kind of promise. Aren't they? And wine,
and noisemakers, and all the little things we thought good at a hinge in space:
     they're
not like that now, are they? And all the kids, and people who came over: now salted
in their time, and we try to break out of ours, I guess, and still the animals
     stampede toward
headquarters. I was depressed when I wrote that. Don't read it. Still, if you must, take
note of certain exemptions in the
fourth paragraph where I was high: they said it shouldn't enter, but I succeeded
     in decoding the big top
so that someday all children should live like this, have what was at last ours,
only I succeeded and a train roared by: *that man,* it seems to say. And then it is past,
after it is flagged down. A sore spot in my memory undoes what I have just written
as fast as I can write; weave, and it shall be unraveled; talk, and the listener
     response
will take your breath away, so it is decreed. And I shall be traveling on
a little farther to a favorite spot of mine, O you'd like it, but no one can go there.
     The mummy
said so. I have to keep in the shadows yet a little longer, until you will wisely see
     how I

fit under here and so must leave any day now.
                                    The boskets were blue, I
        remember; only
a few ships in the distance now, and a tall flag beckons
me in another direction. Dammit, I'll stick to this one, this is the one they meant
for me to take all along, and I don't see why I should take that other one. My child,
you must do as you wish; to do otherwise would insult God's rule, and you do
care for Him, don't you? Only give no thought to the morrow—
it will presently arrive and take care of itself, you'll see. Meanwhile, if a new hat
might seem appropriate, then why not? Oh father I was looking out the window
but this time doesn't seem such a long one, mightn't we return
to the old cabin, just for a glimpse of the driveway? But that,
as the parrot said, is another story. Sooner or later you go blind staring at platinum
and the reverberations that warned against it can themselves no longer be
        distinguished
in the thudding and fog, and if all comes to be eclipsed at some
date in the not-too-near future, then why does it say I'm a salesman with a tie
        trying to
interest you in this new product, that can go out of control? It's the Cotswolds
for me, but no, he has the name tag in his pants and this string flying behind him
into what you were told would be a void, which is his study. Heaven help jerks,
        they need
it worse than we, yet always something funny acts as a short prelude to disaster,
        and then afterwards
everybody is relieved; it's still a high school; there's nothing no longer wrong with it
and the shade acts as a puddle
from which froglike eyes protrude, if it is indeed this occasion, and this is 901½
        McKinstry
Place, and you are Judson L. Whittaker, oh take this wheelbarrow far from my
        sight and bury it

on yonder height, so impatient have my clones become, and I, in the light,
of this new development am all but induced to come along with you. The stones
forbid it though. Fire that does not burn? Tell it to the no longer prematurely
gray slab of expanse, file it in "explanations which leave much unexplained," but
    leave me my
dance, the one underpraised porcelain object on the stand.

In the western districts greetings proliferate
and I'm already starting to look better. When was I not
a paramilitary brother in some sense? Who coined this nickname? For I see
far, in looking, out over a life, the strange, wrenching mess of it, yet which has
some undistressed surfaces and unscaled peaks, or bumps, along with much that
    was fey and
witless as it went by. Where *are* those files now? Is it possible they can have been
    deleted
in the very mouth of time? Grenades pop, rockets vomit their lucklessness into
    the sky,
and which of us wants to bear the responsibility of having looked
something up? which is why
the unplanted cabbages stand tearful out of the mist, there is no
reason to go on ploughing the garden once winter has begun, yet
what else is there to do, except sweep the floor
with automatic hand, pondering certain dun sins of omission, if twilight really is
    a jewel
as you turned out to be (never fear, the rain
won't rob you of your distinctive personality though I saw it streaming
the other day, down your clothes, you paused and seemed not to know what to
    think, but I,

I in my compartment knew: damaged hair, tattered kneecaps, a pimple
or two, and as automatically as one uncloses a window
you filed your report, and the court was amazed, emptied in a moment before
the order of dismissal came. Out of respect I should say I didn't see you very closely;
you were too far down for that, not coinciding with anyone's notion of a
      "person" yet livelier
still for it; oh you showed 'em how to fit into the barrel of an ignored
      idiosyncrasy and
still have room left over for passages of devastating wit that nightly
bring the house down. And if sleep is narrower after that, it's also more pointed,
slanted like the harrow's tooth, to bring up what may be coming along
any second now) and it is, in feathers all over the floor, only now it's the maid's turn
and we may never see what stays groping in her eyes. The floor is lovely, though,
      passionate
and filled with bright ideas like a bride only what it says about us isn't
      forthcoming.
Outside the river is magenta and some sunbeams got caught upside down in it,
      just their
(our) luck I guess. Meanwhile I have received your postcard. I wanted to tell you
how much I thought it shouldn't change, but dairies (diaries?) got in the way
      and exchanged notes
at which time the judgment was all but unreadable, jointures charged with
      embalming fluid,
for it is written that whatever is not glue may be pressed into service as such, and
the trip gets merrier just before a sudden decision is reached concerning the
      child-pests
we thought we'd seen the last of.
                    And for one moment, when apple-dust hangs
in your hair you move that glider over an inch, to be
in shade. Dawn, an egg, comforts one only with the idea of its shape. Later we

are in the round and full of fears: did we confuse that shape
with something else, and if so was it congruent, or like a pair of trousers,
        wavering
in the breeze? And then when you come down to it nobody matters any more.
There is nothing like the old beach. The old tables.
Once, an avalanche of cuties threatened our meeting. Fred bypassed it.
Now the season, "a boundless and festive rejoicement," is on track. I, too, voted for it.
But a subtle form of harassment overtakes, by undermining, each new claim as fast
 as it is put in the docket. Case dismissed. Is it then true that it does not matter,
 or that women give birth to children as easily as a fruit disgorges its seeds?
 Salt in the cure-all dilutes both qualms and unheeded label
  cautions, and when called upon, comes outside in a suit, prepared to play the
        reasonable
inquisitor, listen to shouts. Toward evening a stitch is dropped and the blindly
        desiring
run together like syrup and milk: the only ethos, cranes
severing horizon from water with the great sawing motion that always instills awe
 around wreaths for buddies, and in time your tome will tell them too
 about the never leaving off.
                                Surely that last tragedy will be enough
 and the wind must drop, and it does; a single leaf falls circling,
  alights on the water's swiftly moving mirror as the chorus picks up on hope
  in the black promise facing us. Blood oozing under every door, now tell us
  if we can get this way again by remembering and so turn to glass citizens.
Let the cycle of greed begin again, the sheer poetry of it will win over all but a few
viewers and those servants who choose not to look into the path being proposed
        for all of us
to follow—we'll tell them how—and it has just started to sprinkle
a few seconds ago, just before I arrived here in some confusion but now am
dressing the bare stone, as was long ago ordered,

and can complain, really, of nothing—of my head, square as a box,
receptacle for fools' tools? But it was I who brought them here,
taught them to scratch out a rough living from the soil. Of birdsong or
    caterwauling
in the night? No, I was just living it. Now that it's time for repairs I'm not sure I
had to be brought to the very edge of the indignant abyss, but no matter, if it
    doesn't fly
off on its own, sloth will overtake it, sleep bend the branch to earth.

Yet always in fear of some complaint we adjust dials
to those who lie on their side stricken with the power of the floor, uninhibited;

uninhibited cross farms for gain or planted shapes.
But, "no habitation unless one linger." You were afraid of setting out shoots.

But now that sugared April crosses blink, the shining squalls and yellow
plumes imaginably stuck in hair, and one returns to heaven, under what conditions

does one sort out the waterfall? For always, dark spirits and connivance
underlay the people-mover as it spiraled ever higher beyond

§

the counterpane of colored wooden cows, to the continental divide.
And here one would take some comfort in the waved gesture that told how far
    the sun had shriveled

since we began our climb, the hazards put away under our feet.
"The sun was still high in the heavens," yet a narrow ruffle of flux edged the huge

saucer-like plain, and one began to think of other sets of conditions:
the old people in the house, a long day away; the carbons of pets and other
    mooted toys,

or motion at a stranger in a hat who thinks he knows you from somewhere, but
    it scarcely
matters since you are separating amiably now again, forever, it seems, and the
    clues we

all leave behind are fated not to be found this time,
or if they are it will resemble something a squirrel laid there, a good while ago;
    but since charm can never

§

be quite rinsed from these bones it befits us to go along with it, congratulate it
at last for having had something to say and not said it, as torrents frazzle a canyon

without contributing to its demise unless one chooses to consider inexorably
slow processes that score even the cosmic mind at rarest intervals, and superficially;

secure in the adding up of all things
into a block of hay from which no strand is permitted to extrude.

And while the fire-mind tries out its images on us one last time an unsettling tableau
of doom constructs itself from greenish chalk on the green blackboard, but not yet

for these eyes, while the brandy decanter is bent and yards of cretonne
smother the schoolyard and take their place among the popping trees, yet
        unendorsably, O nargileh.

Long ago the earth rendered this pablum unholy or at least unappetizing.
Then the men began to speak in unison: why not sacrifice something
ordinary, such as a hairnet, and if that doesn't work one can consider what steps
are to be taken, but usually it suffices to

part with some insignificant possession. That leaves nothing to sniff at, later
when details are to be worked out, and as a matter of fact in most cases
the god will make you a gift of it or forget about it, going about his business,
     casehardened,
even as we humans do in strange lands. Of course the troublesome minority of
plaintiffs sometimes chases him back to his hole, and, oddly enough, often
     celebrates this
"triumph" with a drinking feast, little suspecting
how the god likes to wait and catch his enemies off balance, and then, woe to the
     litigious
and even their associates when he hits the comeback trail, nostrils aflare, only
it was funny this time, nobody seemed anxious to stir up hostilities on either side.
A few warning shots were fired, in the air, but even these might easily have been
     produced
by a car backfiring, or random firecrackers—that sort of thing.
Meanwhile the god licks his wounds, fiercely abiding: or so, at any rate, we have
     been taught
to believe, hunkered down in the fallout shelter, awaiting pestilence, a rain of
     arrows, or whatever
the chef may have whipped up for us today.
Yet in fact nothing of the kind has ever happened. We even *feel* pure and not devoid
of merit; our neighbors are nice as pie to us; even strangers salute us decorously
     in the street,
beautifully dressed, for this is indeed a secular feast day.
Shouts, the smoke from campfires almost drown it out. We have almost leveled off;
there is so much to say, but cisterns enclose the precious substance, not much will escape.
Oddly, under giant trees we seem smaller to each other, though the hopes the
     great race kindled
burn even more majestically than before the roll-call
that went on so many centuries to the accompaniment of battle-axes and cats-o'-
     nine-tails,

before such courtesies as we now command became acceptable to that god, the
    dew-weeper, and civilization began to grovel
in the dust for torn sausage-casings and bits of shrimp. But any pedigree
is by definition a long one, so that now it must seem to some called to be
    aristocrats as if
the whole shining night were stitched together to hide their port-wine stains
and even gnomes have some inner sense of nobility that will save the world
when it does begin to fall apart as, at last report, it hadn't yet done, the boiler-plate
contradictions ennobled in it being such as can last millenniums without
    exhibiting the slightest signs of wear,
though we have only ourselves to thank for that. When the convention finally
    assembles
there may be flak to take on that score. In which case we can always plead
    ignorance of the law,
that noblest, since most artless, of defenses, and dig our heels in and ask the cliff
to explain itself and the ferns erupting from its crevices: I too
have stood here faceless and seemingly angry for a long time, yet for all that
don't feel it time to intimidate someone, make him or her feel lonesome just
    because there is
indeed a horizon, but prefer to sit back on my haunches, contemplating my
    navel to see what good
if any will come of it. Frightening noises are in poor taste; silence must be sorted out
however, its path followed back to where the tucks gather, and each random furrow
be gaily explored in a spirit of setting out to conquer the world someday. That's all.
I have no further bread and cheese for you; these days I count little
but the linens folded in my scented cedar closets, folded up against time, in case
I ever have a use for them; and you, you others, have only to break away
like chunks of ice from the much larger iceberg to accomplish your destiny, that
    day in court
the monkeys and jesters seemed to promise you—or was it a bad dream? But
    now, surely,

your mettle has been tested; let the perfume of burning archives
assault our olfactory sense once more as radically as the grape hyacinth in the
     fond gullies of spring.

Access to the poll-takers is limited, yet there are times, I feel, when this artificial
     barrier
along with so many others ought to be rescinded. Once in the booby hatch the
     setting sun
drilled its powerful horizontal rays, as strong as any you'd ever want to see at
     noon, through my
window just above the sill, striking this sheet of paper with the shadows of a
     flower pot
and an old faucet, that were lying there, with so much force that they seemed
     about to be embedded in it,
like a sentiment above a door. At such times, one gathers
that gravity isn't about to save us, that it wasn't installed as some sort of built-in
     smoke alarm
to discourage us from rash actions. We evolve naturally in its aura, there is so much
to say it gets weighted down like a pear tree with fruit, so that when the branch
breaks and the fruit must be harvested at once or discarded, we get stage fright
     and do imitations
of opera singers or anything to break the monotony of the pace
set for us by its metronome. And yes, it's like living in an atmosphere one can
     breathe, but
at the same time one can never take it for granted; like air, it slips by too easily
for anyone to care, once the dust has settled, what that minor commotion
     betokened. The giant
umbrella creations of our history of knowledge have that disconcerting side-
     effect. So one

concentrates on the line tangential to the thick, pebbled bulge of the fruit's skin:
  know it and
one can understand everything's the theory, though in practice
things don't go as smoothly as that. The top of a tower that is visible one minute
may be only a straw blowing across a courtyard the next; so, at any rate, has
  patience, deduction's
handmaid, taught us, and when we go out of doors, we never exhibit bad
  manners or any kind of feeling,
envy in particular. What enters your gate is my own inference, not some
colossal steed pawing the dust in a protracted spasm of preparedness, for what voyage
can any of us undertake until the lotus moon has risen to vanquish
squibs or rumors concerning its eligibility that blew up while one was seated,
  somewhat
taken aback, disinclined to candor that day, or anything that might compromise
  intelligent
speculation about the origin of dreams. So one sees couples
turn back from the altar, it not being quite right for them, and as quickly, cities,
ghouls, ghost ships bite the bullet and plunge from sight, to be resuscitated in
  some more
"normal" atmosphere where telling tall tales comes under the head of bystander
  entertainment,
a special budget item subsumed under crass though meticulous ganders at what
  the staff
has been up to in one's absence, how it looks, what it feels like.
And the dark mahogany
of his mood, how one loved all that! Why is it too late to be simple,
out riding, pointing at something, when all you loved was there anyway? Too late
to be inventoried or caressed, as one lays in a stock of family anecdotes for the future,
poses to assume, frippery, harmless tomfoolery, until in a cocoon
made of commas it will all seem to come right, but the ashes have been left far
  behind

on a nameless road, in whose ruts glass still flashes magisterially,
not merrily short-circuited as when we were among people, but a thing on its
    own now,
to weep over rather than think of saving? If only we could get the message out
    further,
yet here all kinds of sacred cows hinder one, so there is no longer any point
in pursuing the implications today. Tomorrow will be good enough for that.
    The stationary
saraband of our considering it but deciding not to put it to a vote absorbs any
hint of the disorder that highmindedness sometimes trails in its wake like a wisp of
something in the sky, and in any case, our hands, our faces are clean, our plates empty
and brimming with moonlight, a pious reminder to the unwashed and unready
    that we will come
again someday and make sense of this arbitrary and tangled forest of misplaced
motives and other shades of imperfect sympathies that do not compromise us
    perhaps
as yet, yet I feel their aura, Mother, like a water table ascending,
and I haven't the answer, don't know if I'll ever have it, yet it looks so young,
pitiful and hopeless in morning light that one tries to suppress the intuition that to go
forward will be to do battle with some angry titan, sooner or later, and all one's
bad reactions will confront at every one of the house's apertures: slay me and then
leave me here, if that's going to help; just don't stand around
looking at me that way, that's all. Am I some kind of a freak? No. Am I
    disingenuous? Maybe,
but the case hasn't been proved; only an executioner could decide it, and besides
    I feel too well
to get into other feral arrangements when the night and its night-light are still
not far off. And besides other people are too interested right now, the ambiance
    can never
be gauged accurately enough in the feverish commotion that surrounds this, and
    our other

travel plans. There is no point in giving them the slip. It is never too late to mend

no matter how we clamor to redo everything from the ground up; the chatter
    never subsides

but like the tide of dust of the oceans, returns and retreats, forever opaque,
    forever itself:

a longing one does not subdue.

Yet time, for all that, hadn't abandoned

the grotty little amusement park though the wind now seethed through every rent

in its shell, and others now had plans which didn't take it into account:

in the foundry he sang it once and here was this sudden magnificent opportunity

to create a forum, an audience for oneself! Gosh, it's so long ago! Still, one must
    hold back,

feigning disinterest until the proper moment, and then, and then,

it shall fall into our hands and seem what the Lord probably meant for us,
    would have,

without a doubt, if we were known to Him. Which brings up . . . But anyway, it
    would all get

fixed up and then we'd hold a contest and people would learn about it through
    that, and we'd have

more people than we knew what to do with queuing up and asking questions,
    wanting to get involved,

to pledge something, anything, even a nickel a week, it's the thought that counts

and don't you ever forget that. Try sleeping on it. And then we'd have a nice car

and options about things to do; we'd entertain beggars and watch them come
    back for more,

and that's part of the fun, forgetting just what you have done, have given someone, in

the intoxication of your and everyone else's finally winning something in the
    free-for-all

of life just like Betty and your father said, only please don't release it all over me now,
I have to think some. Here, this chair ought to mean something, if I intuit
your philosophy correctly, or maybe it's me, maybe I'm a chair, that's what you
meant isn't it? Swift as a missile the cloud leaves the horizon, rising
in our direction to blanket the city in a minute, and sure, somebody will think
        of something;
sunlight does continue to drizzle on us, but by God we
haven't any right to it, we haven't figured out one thing, and
darkness will too arrive soon and be more unexpectedly lascivious than you
        thought. How do
you wriggle out of the knowledge that we shall all have to answer separately
for our truths if such they are when dying, and meanwhile music wants to take
        the load
off our chests and point the way to a possible recreation period? Oh, but there
        were nights . . .
Your father and I were away much of the time;
it was like not having a home, string, and wads of serge to stuff in the cracks,
yet there were so many of them! I don't wonder now that it all didn't get done,
that practically nothing did, and I don't blame anyone or myself either. At this
        time in one's
life it's permissible not to point the finger, and if we are cautionary, then to hell
        with it.
I'd like some more too yet don't feel I'll get any, and that's OK because I wasn't
        the only one
engaged in tearing down the gnarled structure, exposing the pores of the evidence
for all to see and I won't be the most unsurprised when it rattles and will have
        evidently all
taken place on the sly, at once, and no beekeepers mourn the autumnal splendor
        of our robes
or come to visit when snow stains them with its truth, a truth like another, yet it's
all strangeness, into solitude, and woebegone one sees so little

of what is passing that it's like a show of truth, merely an ad, that spoke volumes
however and would let no one off the hook, even if one were on special
        assignment: that probably
triggered it all anyway. So grouches reform, the day shakes cracked emeralds
        out of its lap
into grooves at the edge of the pavement. Probably this is a true story of how we
        were united.
If so we shouldn't resent ourselves, not until the new moon
has bent its playful bow at least, and this moment too passes with a special
        suddenness, for showing
us what it's like. And other cares will unravel while one is dressing so that the
        differences
more or less cancel each other at the moment of presentation: it's like candy, like a star
that doesn't matter, like one's feet bouncing to a joyful rhythm, a warning next
        time to any who might think of writing.

No one has to re-invent himself at each new encounter with something different
        or slightly new.
Nowhere does it say that results will issue from a recent overhauling.
We don't know what hamlets lie in our path, or how much grumbling will occur
when we knock over something metallic and it makes a loud clang, audible on
        the stairs below,
or whether there will be a comic ending to this. We can see into the future
as into a dimple, and nothing says not to proceed, to go on planning,
though we know this cannot be taken as an authorization, even less as approval
        of the morass
of projects like half-assembled watches, that surrounds us. No but there is a logic
to be used in such situations, and only then: a curl of smoke or fuzziness in
        distant trees

that tempts one down the slope, and sure enough, there is a village, festive
      preparations,
a votive smile on the face of each inhabitant that lets you pass through
unquestioned. And we thought we were lucky back there in the silence! Here,
      civilization takes over,
at its highest, a new trope that dazzles without intimidating, like a scroll, is
      ready for us
and however many more of us it takes to change moods, build the palace of
      reason our
inconsequence has promised for so long now, out of trued granite blocks fired
      with chips of mica,
and so get over feeling oppressed, so as to be able to construct the small song,
      our prayer
at the center of whatever void we may be living in: a romantic, nocturnal place
that must sooner or later go away. At that point we'll have lived, and the having
      done so would
be a passport to a permanent, adjacent future, the adult equivalent of innocence
in a child, or lost sweetness in a remembered fruit: something to tell time by.
By then we'll know, as surely as if parents catechized us, the empty drum that
      offers itself
to any yearning, the daily quotient, the resolution, but also bare facts scattered
      on a plain
of fires, data that cannot be checked, dictates to live by, unlikely as it now seems.
And scattered over these, the dust of heavens that incorporates some of the good
      things and others
you'll most likely want to avoid, if you can, otherwise torpor builds up in plumes
on the horizon, and when you go
to convert your notes into hard currency, something will be lacking though the
      columns
of figures add up correctly, and there seems to be no mystery
to it, beyond a pleasant, slightly numbed sense of wonderment which was in any case

on your original want list. Although we mattered as children, as adults we're
   somehow counterfeit
and not briefed as to what happened in the intervals to which this longing led us,
which turns out to be not so tragic after all, but merely baroque, almost functional.
Yet there can be no safety in numbers: each of us wants and wants to be
in the same way, so that in the end none of us matters, and in different ways
we cannot understand, as though each spoke a different language with enough
   cognates
to make us believe in deafness—*their* deafness—as well as in our own reluctance
to dramatize, leaving our speech just sitting there, unrinsed, untasted, not
   knowing us,
or caring to. Each day the ball is in our court, and worse,
this is probably unromantic and proper procedure, *fons et origo, nemine dissentiente.*

Hours, years later, we were together.
The moon unbarred its hold, the thickness of brambles was compacted
just in time to prevent the closing of the door as if by magic—"It always
happens that way, and then no one can find it. Pretty please,
not in the terrarium, but outdoors, that vague nest,
and others will conspire to push the lawnmower, make coffee, as long as these
and ours are spared and stand along the walk in rows. We might never
get out alive otherwise. Besides, there's all that to see,
all that and more, you see, not including
the glint in someone's eye when you tell them that, and afterwards, well, it's back to
your tunnel or whatever you care to call where it is you stay
in the afternoons, then morning, if all goes well. And if we two inhabit
a daffy teacup, are adept at crowd-pleasing, then what about the rest,
star-gazers in their midst, who make up the electorate? Say it was long ago,
say nothing further need be said, that even a memory will traipse

across the crossed hairs and be shot down, only the comfort in it
will be, will not have been
for many years, and though these die
with a sheen on them there is not very much to mark
of that past, no stones to leave on the trail, which isn't the same
as having an alderman in your living room and cats wherever you look,
fond George."
        Then it said it was supposed to come back
to an eyrie or some sort of enclosed space, it wasn't too clear
about that, but definitely would walk to meet us
whether we were here, or far. It would meet us. And so on. If living
was going to be like that, give me back my clothes, my crown
of gold, and just let me out before I have had a chance to put them on,
regal when partially naked, and you can bet the next one that comes along
will have his say, and then we are gay, and be under a mushroom
the livelong day, because no one wants to play
any more. The mouse ran up the clock, the clock struck one, and it all lurched
into motion again like an ancient conveyor belt an unseen hand flicks on. And trials,
pumpkin-colored ships in the street, disturb the busman's accident long ago,
having no sense of humor, or just barely. The frightened sleep in parks,
though motionless palm fronds announce a quiet evening. You can get over
bouts of humor best by not going indoors
when the moon is full. The lion stood by the bridge
so long it might have been a sculpture, but in the end loped sheepishly away.
And we have to figure out what these coins mean, not knowing the language.

It might be—still, there's no point in being greedy
before one means to—has to—but if it was a game in the beginning
it must be still, despite inertia. It's getting to be the end of a dance marathon

and though people keep cutting in, they do so with an air of resignation.
No point in taking further lessons, just at the moment anyway.
An enormous sense of release hushes the impatience
in the grass, the wayward chirruping about something. One can still stand up,
and that's plenty, under the circumstances. Besides, we'll not leave you alone yet;
the bench you warmed for us looks inviting; soon stars will be out
and you can walk home peering into the distance, hoping
someone will pick us up. Easy now, the stair treads
have come along again, and soon, soon
the bed will drench us with sleep and the surprising leap into the middle of a dream,
striking pennants, pavilions, bringing all natural activity to a halt as it wonders
about this, tests the current, supposes everything
must be OK or we'd have heard. In the next town there's a grist mill and a
    blacksmith,
or was that part of a dream, or did it really exist in a past
one can focus on, extracting its kernel until, like a ship, the shell turns round,
advances on us and speculation is undone for today. And we sobbed into those sails
sometimes, yet the gryphon never wavered until the third blast of a trombone
soothed it and it fell asleep. Now the dangers were tiny ones, but everywhere;
it would have been a good time to stay home, but alas that was a concept
foreign to these steep, peripheral times, these crags like sandpaper
dividing a no-good, swamp-green sky, and all the while
you were just a bit younger, enough to complain and not understand
why all the women stifled sobs and I was appointed to meet you
and bring you to this place, locus of many diagonals
without beginning or end except for the sense of them a place of confluence
provides. So, as is the custom here, I pulled the hood down to cover most of my face.
In a twinkling the mood had changed. The hiatus in the manuscript
buttoned itself up.

        And there were many sets of fraternal twins on earth
to share in a new sense of disparity and reward everyone for what they would have

done anyway, inasmuch as there always comes a time when congratulations fall
just short of the doormat, loved ones are sorely tried, and associates
go blindly about their business, some business at any rate, all to keep the shelving
from imminent collapse by destroying relationships
that were good in the past but have now come to naught
as we see each day in the papers. And if one swoons, another will follow suit
until the entire populace is restive. And surely no one can locate the good in that
except by poring over miles of yellowing folios, which seems unlikely, so it's back
into bed with us again, and that's the way it has to keep happening
for any of us to remain unaware very long of secret provisions and codicils
in the charter it is imperative not to mention—not, you understand, out of a spirit
of fair play but in the ultimate interests of a deeper yet darker strain of being
we have to live toward if anyone is to get any good out of the colossal, foundering
experiment, the braintrust of fiends and werewolves who lie perched just out of
the reach of sleep, ready to reclaim territories surrendered in a moment
of temporary insanity, and others as well that were never in question
until they became bones of contention just seconds ago in the new climate
of sharpened political awareness that hungers always for new victims
like a minotaur, and whose mad thirst for the blood of innocent bystanders can never
be slaked, least of all by tepid gestures toward understanding
seen in a mirror and wrongly interpreted, or lives entirely given over to sacrifice
and austerity, for it is there, cautions the tome, that the greatest losses, the worst
atrocities will be instigated and immediately tallied. For such is the life of a
    young man
these days; there is still time to leave the boat, which at last report
was committed to its moorings, but of course to quit now
would be to miss the whole spectacle, and that, after all, is what
we came for, and shall insist on staying for, once the dirt has settled
and the bats flown back into the trees. And the cicadas stopped stuttering.

§

As dead wood floats, the expanding afternoon exhales
its mousy fragrance, battening on the memory of countless similar
ones it thinks are in the heads of those going about in this one,
and so the structure stands, without any apparent support. Doors are left open
as in spring, and beyond them float tunnel-vision landscapes
brought from somewhere else, and none recognizes the clever substitution.
Here a man carries bags
out to his truck, and makes the same trip over and over. There, windows shine.
And on a far-off hilltop someplace a living sacrifice gleams, red
in the puddled haze, and all eyes are cast downward, defrocked,
speechless. And though one can hear the traffic's swish
as it cuts from one side of the island to the other, one is transfixed,
facing an army of necessary revisions. "How would it be if I said it this way,
or would so-and-so's way be better, easy on the adjectives?" And if I told you
this was your life, not some short story for a contest, how would you react?
Chances are you'd tell me to buzz off and continue writing, except
it's so difficult; we barely begin and paralysis takes over, forcing us out
for a breath of fresh air. Meanwhile the vengeful deity whose acts
are being recorded has all the time in the world. "OK, that's it for today," as if
one weren't busy on other fronts too, such as writing letters
to friends in Panama and Hawaii. Not to mention keeping track of expenses
in a ledger acquired for just this purpose. But though reams of work do get done,
not much listens. I have the feeling my voice is just for me,
that no one else has ever heard it, yet I keep mumbling the litany
of all that has ever happened to me, childish pranks included, and when the
     voluminous
sun sets, its bag full, one can question these and other endeavors silently:
how far wrong did I go? Indeed, one can almost see the answers spelled out
in quires of the sky: Why? it enthuses, and immediately some of the metal trim
falls off, the finish has gotten gooey, but we persevere, and just as the forms
begin to float away like mesmerized smoke, the resolution, or some resolution, occurs.

§

We are no longer on that island. Here, the inmates
treat us harshly, but like adults, and though as usual no rest is authorized,
one can without too much difficulty keep pace with the majority of them
and see one's old clothes reflected in that mirror. And shoots keep popping up;
birds are pecking excitedly in the dirt for something, and your shoes
have grown too small; it will be time to change them soon. Of course, one is too old
to be a waif, yet that issue never surfaces; one is judged fairly
though without this set of complex circumstances being taken into account,
and that's something, more than you think, for by evening
the pronounced moan will have been deadened, and we are free to take our ease,
reveling in the glow, the surface of things, like water nourished on fading light.
You see, we have escaped. But one always goes back voluntarily
before the next roll-call, and that bittersweet dream of complete and utter
laziness is postponed once again, confirmed and postponed. And I write my diary
by street-light, because it's better that way; I may not have to look too closely
at my handwriting, yet I can feel it, all around and on me
like a garment or a sheet, and this too seems like a good idea. Well, doesn't it?

It does. But remember, one isn't obliged to love everything
and everybody, though one ought to try. One way is to accept the face they
present to you, but on consignment. Then you may find yourself falling in love
with the lie, sinister but endearing, they fabricated to win acceptance
for themselves as beings that are crisp and airy, with an un-self-conscious note of
    rightness
or purpose that just fits, and only later take up the guilt behind the façade
in the close, humid rooms of whatever goes down in their struggle (or hundreds

of struggles) against fate, and perhaps buy that too someday
when their manners are out of the way. I have obtained gratifying results in
    both instances
but I know enough not to insist, to keep sifting a mountain of detritus
indefinitely in search of tiny yellow blades of grass. Enough
is surely enough, in spite of what religion teaches us. I'm happy to be back with others
at the fairgrounds, without disparaging them too much, and when someone asks me
what I think of him or her, reply without false naïveté that I really love them
very much, but it might be time to take other factors into account, my own
well-being, for example, and how far along the path to survival my unselfish
instincts have moved me. Usually it's both farther and not as far as we imagine,
i.e., taking a wrong turning and then after a fretful period emerging in some nice
place we didn't know existed, and would never have found without being misled
by the distracted look in someone's eyes. It's mostly green then; the waves are
    peaceful;
rabbits hop here and there. And the landscape you saw from afar, from the tower,
really is miniature, it wasn't the laws of perspective that made it seem so,
but for now one must forgo it in the interests of finding an open, habitable space,
which isn't going to be easy. In fact it's the big problem one was being led
up to all along under the guise of being obliged to look out for oneself
and others: the place isn't hospitable, though it can support itself and one or two
others, but really it would be best to start all over again from the beginning
and find some really decent area that reflects a commitment to oneself.
But where? In a bubble under the surface of the ocean? Isn't it all going to be a
    fiction
anyway, and if so, what does it matter where we decide to settle down?

III

That was the first time you washed your hands,
and how monumental it seems now. Those days the wind blew only from one
    quarter;
one was forced to make snap judgments, though the norms unfolded naturally
    enough,
constructing themselves, and it wasn't until you found yourself inside a huge pen
or panopticon that you realized the story had disappeared like water into desert sand,
although it still continued. I guess that was the time I understood enough
to seize one of the roles and make it mine, and knew what I heard myself saying,
but not whose yellow hair it was. Mélisande? Oh, I'd
come before to let you in, and saw only a chipmunk, and so . . . But now it's nice
to sing along, and read the newspapers together, and try on funny hats: only
be aware that at daybreak there must be no trace of you, or the cock might not crow
and there'd be hell to pay. Besides, you wouldn't wish it
even if we were together, as someday we may be. I say "someday"
for the sound of it, like a drop of water landing, but I also meant it, but now I'm
standing just outside unafraid, listening. So much is wrapped in soot,
that now I'm no longer blind
and can denounce any aggressor, but I won't, because I'm afraid to, and besides,
what if the attic door slammed shut? Much remains unknown
in these calm countries. A bridge erects itself into the sky, all trumpets and
    twisted steel,

but like the torso of a god, too proud to see itself, or lap up
the saving grace of small talk. And when these immense structures go down, no
    one hears:
a puff of smoke is emitted, a flash, and then it's gone,
leaving behind a feeling that something happened there once,
like wind tearing at the current, but no memory and no crying either: it's just
another unit of space reduced to its components. An empty salute.

It's like the wind has taken over,
except that one can be aware of, keep an eye on oneself in that medium:
this one is more like a pock-marked wall, in which spalling occurs due to stress
and anxiety at regular, key points in one's career
(if it can be called that—"progress" is a better word, implying a development
but not necessarily a resolution at the end), and which enfolds you even as you
marvel at its irregular surface before you feel yourself beginning to sink into it,
toes first. Then, usually, one wakes up and everything seems ordinary.
Which is no miracle either, only one's daily ration
of satisfaction after a plenitude of endurance, even as it puts springiness in the gait
and a deceptive, fleeting zest for life until one encounters it again, muddied
and forgotten on the side of a hill above a large city. Which way did they go, it
    wonders,
and horsemen ride up as though on cue, and the rustlers disappear over the ridge,
and the spring trash is freighted with penance yet there is a satisfaction in knowing it
all comes true again and I wave into the flag. How many knives in the corridor
of them one traverses at the rate of one inch per minute, and do those in charge know
what to do with them? Do they even know where they are? Not at the last
    point where speech coincided
with the much-embraced hem of someone's robe as it swept by too fast for
    compliments

to occur in near-zero-degree temperature with a wind-chill factor of minus 51
   degrees Fahrenheit
but too slow for cognitions relative to our positive but neutral, spreadeagled stance
re the conniption chambers of this world and our frequent encounters with them,
give or take a year or two, and then it's gone, again. There was no one to tell us
   what it meant
when it meant what it did; we had to rely on quasi-secret details of costume encoded
into the larger blank that would do us harm but remains stalled off the coast, O
sister of my worst enemy, to know how it talked back to us when we were no
   longer there
to receive the ice cream and the short shrift, but when we did get back there was
   nothing
but a well-dressed old gentleman waiting in the lobby who told us we ought to apply
for an emigration visa but did nothing to help us solve the vexed question of
   directions,
oil the bureaucratic wheels; thus in one kind of mess one dreams of others, perhaps
more serious, but which have the attraction of occupying the middle distance;
   meanwhile
all the porters have shuffled away, under the erroneous impression we haven't
   the coin
to pay them no doubt, yet it's not true, we would pay them if we could, but just look
how they have left the funhouse mirror clearly visible for perhaps the first time
and we can at last admire our billowing hips and hourglass waists through which
the background music of the street pours at an exponential rate, quite enough
to deafen less serious characters than we, who benefit from being put in our place
without imagining the successes with which we were daubed in earliest
   childhood
and which continue to stick to us long after they have worn off
in the eyes of some, preachers and paupers alike, but did it ever occur to them
   we aren't
as they imagine us, or even as we imagine ourselves, but more like bales

of hay, already harvested but still sitting around, waiting for someone to put them
in the barn before rain and rodents have their way with them? Surely, no one
creeps, no one speaks, yet one can't call this silence,
there are too many ships on the horizon, and besides, a pea
blinded me the last time I tried to look for significance in it, and then lots
of people are ready to tell you you've gone astray, but what about the rest of them:
they may not think so, although they say nothing. Our words are interpreted left
and right as they become speech, and so it is possible at the end that a judgment
    may be
formed, and yet the intrepid
listener does no such thing, hypnotized by his reflection, and it is up
to us to file the final report on the decision in many cases. As flax is blue,
I desire your toes, and in the final
harbor our destinies though parallel are too closely linked to be seen as such, my
boulder that rushes to me yet hangs suspended
like mistletoe and we all go often to a place we are familiar with,
though it seems strange and uncompromising. So much was I taken aback by
the rules of the prostitute, it seemed for a while we should never reach the oval lake's
opposite shore, but then we did, suddenly; it was like looking for a lost object
and finding it in the palm of your hand. Out of the sad spring, no heart-
    clenching chime
then or ever; the development was muted, then fudged; but one had been
    warned to play
within the enclosure on the off chance that something slightly singular would
    occur; this
took the form of accidental meetings with old acquaintances. Never mind, it
    said, about how to
give dignitaries the slip; your job is to play with responses, until, elsewhere, they
    are changed
to raw greetings and obtuse expressions about how this or that influenced one's
    gradual ascent

to greatness with not so much as a look back in any direction, and when these
    "come true,"
when the future has arrived, not be the last to put in your consent to what, in
    actual fact,
transpired long ago when noses were buried in manuscripts and lampshades
ornamented our own landscape quite sufficiently, or so it is claimed in reference
works by forgotten but reliable authorities. The sheen, like that of silk, on the
    night air,
and the days, plain old miserable days scanned by a gas engine's rattle, or, worse,
afternoons in a canoe, with the quality of rebounding off yourself as you write
in water the name of the beloved, and later get a chance to see it on vellum, in
    blood-red.
No task actually kept us here; besides it was much too airy, but I want
to single out certain elements in the role indifference played in all our lives,
    winding down
toward a town that continues to hold our attention
after seven centuries of interaction of the divine with the sparse sentinels, posted
here and there, of our attention to portents high and low issued from a cave
on the edge of Main Street and therefore able to transport us instantaneously to
    the region
of whatever happens to be interesting to six or more people just then: a steeply
    shelving
lawn purplish with black gargoyle-like shadows and lesser animadversions,
    weak though sincere
ones, and we have to get off here, it's our stop. But we *will* come back, no question
of it, some other time when all the right numbers have come up, conflated with
    calls for
truth and decency at whatever street corners they may abound: so is it likened
    by clerics
to what had never gone before, except to say, I still love you. The barn has begun
to tarnish and it would not do to stay any longer, even though you were posted here:

it is essential that you leave this very evening, that you not look back
or ever give a thought to the circumstances that transported you to this place
of easy definitions and only so-so resolutions, because all
that was going to name you has been shunted aside, and it beseems us to act
      modest in turn, lest
our very lack of success be turned into an accusation of failure, and the loved things
spiral off to the rungs of distance, as the sandpiper pecks at the shore when the
      sea rushes out.
The panel impelled consideration of the question. So sure there are some that
      stay home
and mope, taking the path of least resistance, as
their dreams go to the opera and out to supper afterward, having a marvelous
      time, one
imagines, coming home at dawn. But for all the good this does anyone, ask the
      fairies,
and the record is eloquent on this point: no fire sales, none at all, before the end
of friendship. It was the day-to-day banter, you see. Besides, whose business is it if
      none
of us turns up, we signed no agreement, life gets along quite well without us, don't
you suppose, and if the sky is rarely green at evening, the water often is, when there is
an overlay of gold leaf and nothing too disgusting shreds one's patience as it did
the last time these books were taken out. Really, my dear, I
don't see any point in disturbing people about a few pencil-shavings on the desk-top
any more than your dead tea-leaves annoy *me*. Why then, should people swing
      toward people
in groups, and when some collide and others keep on going, misstate the occasion?
Either it's a social event or it isn't. You can't get away
with having two kinds of activity back to back: it just won't work. Otherwise
we'd all be happy, or blissfully out of our minds is more like it, but work
has to get done in the cracks, joists be visible, for it to matter, and happen: you know
the shed was bare in the morning, and when you crept back to it at noon, it still was

and was obviously going to be again when twilight arrived, broom in hand.
    Now the shocked clocks
jangle otherwise, but back there, when it was doing its being, who thought
    about time?
Who cared about being caught red-handed when there was so much to hear and
    complain about,
so many bodies sitting in drafts, backs bared for our added enjoyment when
    a man with a pipe
tiptoes in, and abruptly one felt uneasy, one's mood blunted by this seemingly
    unrelated
conundrum. It was then we got up to go. One simply stormed out of the
    baroque palace
in arctic weather, clad in a filmy negligee, with no thought for the morrow,
not the least concern for where cash or food were going to come from. Call it a
    happy ending,
there is much to praise in a decidedly mixed climate of coming-of-age films and old
bear masks, one would say, especially insofar as the current underlying it was cool,
not having made up its mind yet. The few who did escape were considered dangerous
and were put down, so that for a long time there was no really reliable account
    of what went on
in there: besides, who knew? Even belated guests having fun in a fit of champagne
and ruled legal paper were undercut by their own memories of what this would
    have been
in a past that can make no sense to them, now. Besides, if *you* said it one of them
    might obey
and there would be an end of it. Can you imagine? Nothing but ecstatic rooms,
one after the other, and strong possibilities of *becoming* one's desire and thereby
mastering it and one's own plans for the future before they begin to drift,
causing the consternation that we know. Come to think of it, why couldn't we
    all play at
savoring how the sun seems to grow aware of us gradually, until late in the evening

when one is excused, and can go and write down one's impressions? At least,
I thought that's what it was all about. You may contradict me, but I *see* life
in the dead leaves beginning to blow across the carpet, paraffin skies, the beetle's
    forlorn
wail, and all at once it recognizes me, I am valid again, the chapter can close
and later be mounted, as though on a stage or in an album. Really not too much
    does get
left out, if you count it to the end, not including the hopes and desires that intervened
and made you think of it, but only the smooth moments that were ours, *O*
don fatale, as someone said, and I agree, and now I must post this, feeling you
in my hands and along my arms, as though it were all going to stop and begin
a few minutes after the alarm sounded. Much of it is there, intact and around.
Someone could start it up again. I know. We were all cute kids once.
Lately I have this feeling you were avoiding me. We could sum it all up as a bunch
of nerves, little people peeing around, but there goes my Doberman's tether, he's
    off and running,
not to put too fine a point on it. And the cooling-off period ended, dirty,
this time. As these strangers of our waking existence are consumed, their
    outlines darken
and are suddenly stronger. We'll never get rid of them. They erupt as you start
    to move,
become your belt or maxim, ride roughshod over the ancient imperatives,
and there is nothing to see. You are inside the box. It couldn't have happened
in a more convenient interval. Yet life
is after all very much what they are all about:
why drag it out, sniff and whine, merely to remain perpendicular
to the afterlife, buying that notion. Visions at sea: the old promontories are there,
an argument I had with my father, the store that sells antique tools, and only a little
about cleaning up my act, really sitting down and just doing the job. Then the
    abandoned
projects need pampering too. So I walk out into the street, wearing a shirt,

and buy something. And the cake is eaten. No crumb is left over. There were
    never going to
be any, since what was predicted has already happened. You can turn off that
    appetite now.

Girls, I don't know, there were a lot of them but no special one.
Boys handed cigarettes around.
The newspaper had just hit the stands. The airplane was mentioned in it.

No one had come to shake hands. Besides they were just walking. A basin or
    two. That
shattering discharge of light just when sunset is supposed to occur, striking
terror into your heart, but gone the next moment. To be born eclectic is, I
    suppose, to die
into my idea of what you are, a basso-profundo fibrillation, an idea like a pit.
Here, I can't hold it up by myself, you've got to help. One can, one does exist like this
but what a thin home it makes. No place to put my despair. Never mind, we'll
    unpack it later.
Meanwhile I haven't told you what the kids said
about the airplane, and how their place on it was nice. Lots of people told stories.
It was grand, a truly grand homecoming: lifers off the sauce, raccoons that
    dodge, cheese
and pastry for everybody, canons praised, until the knife came
and sat on the chopping block, which was a bit problematical, but we figured
    out a way
to include it in our rounds, so it never got bored or lonesome. The bigger
    children had fits.

Soon all was gray, and gay. Honeybunch had never seen
so many distasteful lives intertwined, and Mary Ellen hadn't either. When the
    fray comes
undone, and the world is a frump, why it's time to make hay in the rain, leaving
the door closed, that tells its own story: a world of pimps, a season on a pink beach,
mauve twilights that plop down on you in the tropics and then ask *you* the way
    out, insist
on the recipe—still, one could have a fine time or two,
then. We were younger, but not as rich. By the time we were old, everyone cared,
and it was time to try something new, but the wine had taken over, what was
    supposed to be a lark
ended in the dark, and then how do you count them? The waivers, I mean
the insects, in the bloody awful place you brought me to. I suppose I could
    forgive you,
given the era, but then they all shouted. It was supposed to be embarrassing for me,
coming back, I mean. So I just put on the halter and waited, for what seemed
like tall summer afternoons, and a breeze came and kissed me on the head, and I
    was out of it,
finally, free to collect my things—you know how that feels. So I swaggered
over to the bar, was refused admission. Then I lay on my back in the street
for a while, gazing up at the stars, but soon tired of that too. So I got up, traded
    places
with a beggar standing next to me, and set out in rags to see the world itself,
a pretty tired place by that time. And so arrived home without further incident,
    "the trip
was uneventful," as they say, except in between I need more time with you, and
    primroses,
which I collect. There was a bad day too at school, but you see this
no longer concerns me, I am kind of semi-retired now, and don't wish to go
    pushing people
or putting on airs. Some of the young people came to stay. It was lovely, then.

§

But I'll tell you one thing: it wasn't easy. Mornings, I'd be at the library
while it was still dark outside, straining my eyes over useless newsprint, all
in the interests of some dumb theory I was trying to prove,
even after I'd forgotten what it was. There'd be times I thought I'd hit on
    something—
eureka! And then I'd realize I'd ignored an important bit of chronology, for instance
that A and B weren't even alive during the same century, and I'd be forced to
    backtrack,
treading water, then as always. Sometimes an important fact would come to light
only to reveal itself as someone else's discovery, while I felt my brain getting chafed
as everything in the reading room took on an unreal, somber aspect. But outside,
    the streetscape
always looked refreshingly right, as though scene-painters had been at work,
    and then,
at such moments, it was truly a pleasure to walk along, surprised yet not too surprised
by every new, dimpled vista. People would smile at me, as though we shared
    some pleasant
secret, or a tree would swoon into its fragrance, like a freshly unwrapped bouquet
from the florist's. I knew then that nature was my friend. "We do it," the
    contractor said,
"routinely." And sure enough, it was as though everything were posing for a
    photographer,
helping you to get the right angle. A snowy panorama would automatically
    appear framed
by a lych-gate; parked cars would reveal carved wooden heads, of unknown
    origin, affixed
to the house behind them. Beautiful girls wearing peasant aprons would sink,
    laughing,

in a circle on the grass, one of them tilting her head thoughtfully upward
as she chewed on a spear of hay. You can bet this helped me along with my
     work. Or if
the water in a vase appeared clouded, someone would have replaced it
the next time you noticed, and gone on to other happy, thankless tasks. I kept
     my counsel
as I continued to write, and then, because that is the way I do it, would greet
or compliment someone when they weren't expecting it, and you know
     something—I do it
because they expect me to, and that's the way I want everything to be. Because when
darkness does come we'll need advice, and the only way we'll get it is by looking
     at what
we wrote down a long time ago, thinking it of no importance and laying it
in a shallow box or drawer. But when you do really need to know the essential
nature of a thing, recognize it by its texture only, the cup by the handle, the gas
from its sudden volatility, you'll be glad you
wasted so much time in youth jotting down seemingly unrelated random
     characteristics of things,
rested on your elbows at the windowsill looking out over everything that was
     going to be night,
as dismay took two steps backward into curiosity and brought momentary relief
     in the form
of an incorrect solution that might be read later on as a stain
on your record, before everything became justified by age, antiquity
having usurped a moral force hitherto in suspension, now focused
on all the manifold exploits of men and animals. And not a moment too soon—
     the page
that was waiting to be turned had grown heavy as a barren mountain range, and
     armies
of civil engineers equipped with the latest in pulleys, winches, sprockets and
     windlasses

were just at that moment attempting to negotiate its sheer sides, with little success,
until in your sleep you muttered the word that released them, it sank, and all
    returned
to normal for a while. Music had gotten caught in the chinks of their argument,
that is, their history: it too disengaged itself and flew off, lapwing-wise, into the air
and the sun came out as though to congratulate earth on the felicitous result which
might so easily have proved far other, setting the race to humanity back a couple
    of hundred
years. At such times we are allies, rejoicing to feel the firm pavement under our feet.
And when things stagnate we can easily stir them up to produce an evocation
of freshness, until the next major change is called for. You'd better believe we can
bestir ourselves when necessary, though leisure is always productive, too,
leading, at the end, to truths it was never possible to envisage, or, even now, to
    formulate.
Let the weather of it all wash over me like a wall, I am not foolish, only a little
fanatical, but I do not intend to let that hinder me or discourage all of us
from taking ourselves down a peg, if needful; I have only the world to ask for, and,
when granted, to return to its pedestal, sealed, resolved, restful, a thing
of magic enmity no longer, an object merely, but one that watches us
secretly, and if necessary guides us
through the passes, the deserts, the windswept tumult that is to be our home
once we have penetrated it successfully, and all else has been laid to rest.

And the river threaded its way as best it could through sharp obstacles and was
    sometimes not there
and was triumphal for a few moments at the end. I put my youth and middle
    age into it,
and what else? Whatever happened to be around, at a given moment, for that is
    the best

we have; no one can refuse it, and, by the same token, everyone must accept it,
for it is like a kind of music that comes in sideways and afterwards you aren't sure
if you heard it or not, but its effects will be noticed later on, perhaps in
people you never heard of, who migrated to other parts of the country
and established families and businesses there. Yet sometimes too it'd seem like
     a moraine,
filled with rocks and bloom, a mammoth postscript
to whatever you thought your life had been before.
At no time did the music seem remotely interesting. You must always keep
     listening, though,
otherwise you might miss out on something. And there is something lovely
about haunting voices filling the high vaults of a basilica:
just the idea that they want to sing leads to a fork in the path,
and that can never be used against you because there are already far too many old men
to count as a reproach, with downcast eyes,
following the path wherever it leads now. Besides, it's impossible to be young enough
anyway, and the leaping intervals of the music don't so much consecrate
     youthful hopefulness
as excuse the follies of old age, as, running around like chickens with our heads cut off,
we try to excommunicate everyone including ourselves from society: even the
     word "society"
is something each of us eventually gets a stranglehold on, forcing it to say
     "uncle"—there,
I'm glad I did, and you can go away now. Such are dried fruits, a pleasant treat
perhaps in some afternoon that can be, but as I sit here it doesn't seem anything
can establish itself as the slab of meaning I feel central to my situation and all unwary,
unprepared to do anything. Looking out at the bay
one imagined one had seen it before.

§

Did I say that thing to you? I hope not—
but if I did, please forgive me—it wasn't the real me, but in any case
we have to get on with our lives somewhat, make swift compromises
for all the world to see, and sparrows fly off, and it shall be as perhaps it was before
when night tickled the very notion of seeing without artificial light, and finally
it began to rain past thirst, past any notion of seedlings, of decay, of posterity
and protocol, wherever they have fled now. Beyond horses and the island.
It would all be just as you were going to have it in a moment. No boys unloaded then.
The poor sailor seeking the familiar is still lost, and no one appears to know
anything about our circumstances. At least until we have been coaxed past the limit
of civilized performance. All else fades. Here is my pen. I am resolved to write
no more, until this business be settled, one day or the other. Cancel all my
        appointments.
Remember to water the dieffenbachia. And please, curl your hair. It's getting
        stretched-
looking. There are biscuits in a container under the counter. Otherwise, why
it's plenty being out in the air and watching others run. Someone came down
from upstate to see me, and that was fine. We rummaged in drawers for a spell.
        My, how
that bush has grown. Aren't you tempted too in the sweet part of the night
to give up your secret by whispering it and then roll over,
convinced nothing can ever repair the climate? And when, in the morning,
        everything
suddenly looks so frighteningly reassuring, and you automatically reach for the note
on the night table and find it gone, is this despair because it meshed better,
or is it all just animals in tall grasses, not so much as a sapling on the horizon,
that is one we have never seen before, though it all looks
like something I saw once in a waking dream, in Minnesota, perhaps? And you
        find you can't
add any more; somebody starts to sympathize and that frightens you, you run away
for a while, then stop and rest,

because where could you get to, anyway? Only if *he* authorized it, which is unlikely,
will we ever see those towering organ-pipe cactuses like deco skyscrapers in a city
one always wanted to live in, but if he comes back maybe he'll do something
about all the others who pestered an infant once, and, when it was time to go,
didn't say they'd had a nice time or anything. If, indeed, I am findable under the lens
of this disinterested red-haired scientist, and if he is willing to exchange me for
a hostage, why then I will go, no question of it. If, however, it is only to force me
to "take my medicine," then I'll stay. It's that simple. It's decided. We
have no way of forcing others to cooperate except by vaguely acquiescing
to their most intimate desires and pretending we don't know what it's all about,
    what
we are doing, and who are they? I thought one was the milkman. But it doesn't
matter because while still enrolled in a course at a local community college I
    happened
once to overhear a conversation between two boys in the next row of lockers, and it
sounded, well, suspicious. I thought I should tell somebody something, and ran out,
but the office was closed, although it was only a little after four, and a tremendous
black bruise stood up in the sky. This was definitely not something to kid about,
I thought as I ran the few blocks to a stationery store, which was closed too—damn!
No wonder kids can't get their schoolwork done. And then I noticed every
    window in every
single-story house was like an eye with a trembling eyelid, and knew that the hour
had come to deliver my speech, and did, the gist of it being: where, assuming
it can be located at all, when you came from the well, gingerly
making your way along the low masonry wall in the side of the bluff, did you
    expect the others
to be, if not in the roofless enclosure they called a house and were planning to
    enlarge
someday? Why didn't Dad reach for his shotgun then, instead
of putting some of them out of the house and grabbing the others and forcing
    them back

inside? Another roll of the glass paperweight and snow shoots up
out of the sagebrush, engulfing the bunkhouse: now see
here, is this what you ordered the man to be? Not if you have a warrant,
it isn't, and can't be exchanged or refunded, its name is a great hiss of waters
rolling toward, then past us. And just see how
the fire ants got washed away, in a red cloud on the surface of the billows,
their mandibles pawing the air pathetically, since after all it was the life force
that impelled them, as it does us, and now they are gone, and we have lasted
but are no better for it. Shit, let's go home. I mean, I forgot my key.
And the road has no survivors. They are probably with him in the jeep up ahead.
One dives at one, then at another, asking, beseeching an explanation
that is not forthcoming. If they were my kids, I'd discipline them different
but nobody can predict, when the day's work is done,
how much vomit would cover the stone surface and where you'd get 'em even
        if you had 'em.
Nice boys at school. It don't do much to mess with the vegetation leastwise
when it clambers like this and could be leaves or part of a tree
or a house in a miniseries. Therefore all ends in disappointment. And if you did
good that's fine, but if you did bad it don't make no difference, you're equal
same as the others, and the devil don't give a shit who you are
or whether your name has an umlaut to it. But we can rest, smooth from the
        attack,
until wit returns, and you shine
the little copper ring and something good will come of it. Few, however,
were interested in doing so, because of having already done it, and nothing
behind them. One little scholar however did observe
how odd it was to see two people here—you see, no one told
us about other names being on the list. It was, in effect, highly unusual,
though no more so than circumstantial evidence or grass being covered up. Here
a moral dilemma socks one: is it better to remain single, conscious of the many
overlapping half-lives that with luck add up to one, or should

we be planted at many listening posts ready to radio vital information back to
    whoever
stands at the long bar? And will my genuine if respectful indifference militate
against the neutrality of my performance? Is a conflict of interest shaping up, or
    what?
Or will these woolly, ball-like constituents of my flock teeter
permanently on the edge of forgiveness, of having something to say
even when I'm down the fire stairs preparing to exit into the alley, before losing
myself in the turbid flood of passersby that wearily
accosts one in the major thoroughfare it empties into? People that look like the
    Gov and Min
in a more strained version: the colors are soiled even when the long coats are clean,
and move swiftly past to tea or some such tropical rendezvous.
They've had it with us, seems to be the universal psalm emanating from some
    debris' psaltery:
and anyway, who dat man wid de fish? Is he the one who must drive death's
    wagon for a year
until somebody else dies and has to take over the job? (And how spidery the *attelage*,
the incomplete wheels.) Oh we must be ever saying and sighing
until what's-its-name gets you up there again, to turn the ever-accomplished phrases
once more and file out having been paid; then there's an argument, a stout
    middle-aged woman accuses a
weasely person of trying to grab her handbag and all hell breaks loose:
fat Irish policemen in outdated uniforms frantically blow on tin whistles until
a phantom paddy wagon drawn by six slavering horses careens down the
    narrow, muddied street.
It's all over for today; you can go home. Wait, the woman
still wants to know about her change purse; it wasn't in the retrieved handbag.
Things go from bad to worse; it sickens one when one
thinks about it for a second; yet having to explain to one's kindly interlocutor
that it's the crisis of humanity, not this isolated incident, is a fate worse than death,

almost. Here, we can duck into this café. You'll feel better
in a moment, but it's best not to take these things too seriously,
not be so thin-skinned. Honest. A rose is blowing over there. The baker comes
    out of his shop
and smiles, rubbing his hands on his floury apron, and the wind
picked up the veil off that woman's face and revealed her beauty
before she hastily jammed the hat down over her forehead and trotted swiftly off.
O my fellow members in the secret society, do you see what secrecy has brought
    us to,
do you know that shad are running in the river, that dams are collapsing in Italy,
and about other fields of interest? For me, it's not so much enough that someone
    brought me
here to my senses, as that the recent past is almost dead, that some other
people, though no officials, have struggled to greet me despite the dust storm's
increased severity, that no tax can ever be legitimately imposed on this period
of my uncertainty, that a score of bloopers hasn't imperiled my career—yet.
And that these elements combine thrillingly, almost diabolically, to
disarm the cryptogram, making us all well again in each other's arms, for as long
as one fancies time or happiness endures—check one. Well I see I've
not outstayed my welcome, that on the contrary quite a few people are waiting
in the anteroom to shake my hand. And with this reassurance, nothing ever
    quite seems
complete again. Yet it isn't exasperating. No furniture-bashing please.
And as we congregate this way, the actual lists of heaven seem roseate
anew. Flames lick the pulpit. This is the way to go—here. This the place
to be.

IV

I had
many ties to the region. And yes, life has a way of sidling on in rain-slick afternoons
like this as though nothing were amiss, as though we had just
seen each other five minutes ago and that tantrum was all for naught. As for the
     rusted
tackle on the rickety wooden dock, that's hardly our affair, is it? Is it
even worth the bother of trying to locate the owner? Think about the mountains,
their motto, "We grow the best for all the rest," and then ask yourself why it is
     you fall
out with those you love most, saving the look on your face for casual
     acquaintances, or,
better yet, complete strangers who are still pure and unrewarded: such society
as the place afforded, and as I took my seat among them, knew it wasn't my
     lot to be privy
to barbs and conversations about tilefish such as this, but would hold on for a time,
as tomorrow beckoned, and today would soon be then. And minutes still trail
by, loitering. As my cock hardens I can make out a group of primitive wattled
     structures
just below the horizon, and am allowed to wonder why, in such circumstances,
     anybody
would want to live from one day to the next, without assurances, no sketch
or dream of the morrow, and then it's gone. It disappears from view.

Patiently you again show me my name in the register where I wrote it.
But I'll be off now, there's no point in thanking me for what I haven't done, nor in
my thanking you for all the things you did for me, the good things and the less good.
In riper times of trial we stayed together. But in this kind of bleached-out crisis-
feeling, the best one can do is remain polite while dreaming of revenge in
     another key, even
with a different cast of characters who know nothing of the life you came from,
that neat trajectory that gradually became confused and later submerged in
     th'encroaching
gloom of everybody's opinion of what you should do to prevent it.

I suppose it does congeal slowly, like those footprints a primate
made one morning zillions of years ago, and that says *something* about spontaneity
as well as one's right to privacy. It's not like it was fused in a furnace;
it slowly ebbed into its permanent state just by appearing every so often
unchallenged; its absences too were seldom commented on, even as they grew
     less infrequent,
so that it became one's privileged daily routine without anyone's being the wiser.
The man told us that first-off. No one can plead ignorance, therefore,
and any other plea-bargain seems out of the question, though my
backers will tell you otherwise. And I can see no outcome but further fractioning
as precious time elapses, and a totally unexpected split decision that benefits no one
 except perhaps those it lulls to sleep with promises of "good times"
long after its half-truths have been assimilated by the rabble it now seeks to contain
with only partial success. Our love, that we didn't know about, mitigated
our reception at the outset; the misunderstanding could only grow, so that it seems
desolation and solitude were the point we had set out for, the times of mirth
forgotten now, recorded in disappearing ink that doesn't outlast winter
and its holidays, its occasions. If I said to you now, let's go out somewhere, you know

what you would think; it's hardly worth disturbing even the sour calm of
    whatever fell
from day to day, like a croquet ball tentatively negotiating a stair, all cakes and
    notions
of pleasure screened by the past, the evergreens that shot up
in the twenty years you were away. Does it look like
I care now, that it matters still? Or is it the calm
of a moment of eternity, not something one lives in, fusses over, but only builds?
I must ask you to leave now. It seems we are fresh out of turnips.
The big spider of the day is broken. Who could repair it?
"Whatever things men are doing shall germ
the motley subject of my page." And that shall leave a great deal after it
in the way of trails. Besides, as trails go, we are pretty incompetent
except to watch the sun slide away, and the trellis of clouds
with it, while the city's modest spires stay put, again, as usual.
The madhouse statuary seemed to dispel the pre-life we gave it
in sleep, to become the one bauble rescued from that hoard, whose shapes
no one now will know. It cannot be said they existed. Yet
surely there was life once in those seams, life the daughters of the iron teeth
of time gave it, and swallows flew over it. One might say, casually,
that there was variation in it, that there was texture. More, though,
one still couldn't say. Yet one day the sanitation department decreed
it was coming through, a nice day in May with the usual blossoms, though these
were only accessories, having no bearing on the tale or
its context, petal-like, in fact, like a cat's nose, but the judge
happened by just then and told them to stop it. They went away and someone,
a bushy-haired man, came back and said it was OK, they could keep on doing it
if they wanted to, but not to say he said so, but that it was OK.
I long meanwhile for the confines of any other principality, but can't abandon
working even if I wanted to, it's like play to me though I get no pleasure from it
except pausing at odd moments to watch the rill for a few seconds,

and then it's back to work again, more work, lots of it, and the pollution
attendant on it, like Hebe to the rainbow's gauzy showers, or web, and I
can't stand on tradition nor beside it. Here it suits me, boys, to turn
over a new leaf like a chunk of recalcitrant granite. I know no other gadfly
who berates me so much; I love it; the woman came back to say she was in the way
and would we go away please it was four o'clock. Not on your life thundered the
hangman, and so it became a kind of ritual, then a game, and every day
someone came to ask after the stone, and someone would stand up to say
it has gone away, go lose yourself in studies or the wilderness;
more none can say. He just came up that day,
had a look round, and left. We aren't even sure
we saw him. It could have been wildflowers in the wallpaper
or stray ashes in the grate, no more. Then the bird came back and shat
on the stone, and that proved it was there for a while, but somehow
that got forgotten and we were thrust out of doors to play in the rain
and sleet, and somebody got hold of the key, we entered, and presto, no one
was there, it was a different room, another empty one too, and had
obviously been vacated pretty recently. A smell of kippers
hung in the front hall. OK, I said, we must press on to the last house
they were seen in in the next block. The green cement one. But my
companions whispered why, let's ditch him at the first opportunity, no
let's not even wait that long, which is why I came across the lawn bruised
and moist, and trembling with pity to be let in, and you came
and let me in. Nowhere did I have anything to say again, but that
was not noticed until yesterday, too late to have us do anything about it.
One source said it was the tulips, against the nice gesture to be led and fed
and have others shut up about it. But one said, you can't have that
and not condone the listless others who don't know yet they're walking
in your tracks and will be sorry when they find out, but another man joined
the woman and said you could too talk about it, it was just a subject
and therefore forgotten, i.e. dead. And Joan she said

too it was like being dead only she didn't care, she might as well be anyway, for all
she cared, and then someone came back with beef. And said here
put a rose on this, you're not afraid, you do it, and someone said, O if the law
decree it he must do it. So the one went in and the others stayed out and waited.
And if you're not going to do it, and if it's none of your business, why are
you going to do it, the first one said, to which that one said: begone. You are my
business in any case and it behooves me not to be in the shadow of you
while I wait. And then one who came from a great distance said, why does it suit you
to be ornery, if others cannot join the general purgative exodus, to which that
    one inside
said, and so it becomes you, if it become you. And then in the shade they put
    their heads
together, and one comes back, the others being a little way off, and says, who
do you think taught you to disobey in the first place? And he says, my father.
And at that they were all struck dumb
and left that place falling all over each other
in their haste to get away, and it was all over for that day.
But another day came and the rice was still laying
on the ground, next to the dust ball. And one took it up, saying,
this is all that shall be till I get back from my trip.
And the others were amused because he had never mentioned a trip before,
but he spat at them, saying, you are too powerful now for my injunction to take hold,
but just wait till the others see you in my chamois costume, because if you think
    it's too late
now what will you think when it has gotten really out of hand
like a vine that grows and grows and cannot stop growing, or a fire
deep in a coal mine that burns for centuries before anyone can do anything
about it. So he stepped down at last. And the others, charred
and unrecognizable, concurred that something extraordinary had taken place
    and that there
was nothing to be done about it. And so he went away.

§

Love that lasts a minute like a filter
on a faucet, love that is always like headlights in the glistening dark, heed
the pen's screech. Do not read what is written. In time
it too shall become incoherent but for the time being it is good
just to tamper with it and be off, lest someone see you. And when this veil
of twisted creeper is parted, and the listing tundra is revealed
behind it, say why you had come to say it: the divorce. The no reason, as
the plane dives up into the sky and is lost. All that one had so carefully polished
and preserved, arranged in rows, boasted modestly to the neighbors about,
is gone and there is nothing, repeat nothing, to take its place. Only should we
wander a bit and then return without expectations, does some faint impulse
    twitch at its
base before expiring, and a lesbian truth rise up for a split second, and the faint
material truth dies again, and then flickers like a post-mortem arrangement
until the rabble of the skies cries and all is assumed to be productive.
Get your ass out of here. But it is time
to work again, but a sad, a tragic time, a time of trifles
and vast snowbanks, and so
you put on your hat backwards and decipher it again dutifully; it's the home stretch
but dare I say more before you think it's time to go and they think so
but they say only, is no more time to stay *here*, in any case we would have gone
if we knew where to go, but we have a place to go, so we will go there. And behind
the barn it behooves us again to take up the principle, so like the art
of tragedy and so unlike, and so we let it rest carefully, and someone says
he would like to be off, and the others agree, it ignites a general stampede
before the clock closes down. In the old corners of why the situation
was ever allowed to come into existence in the first place, the nasal whining

is first heard, then perturbed groans and idle retreats into shuttered
middle distances and auxiliary alcoves. Aw, shucks, someone
seems to be repeating, we could stay here all night if we wanted to
but that couldn't bring the child back into being, and I say, I suppose so.
One's gone for some grants. Be back
when the coal trestle is finished, and idle
against the apricot lamé of the distance here. And boys I know
the distance between your empty bellies and the jobs that will not fill them,
but I still maintain you are better here, but better off far from here
where the choo-choo whistles and a deadly white wind stoops to take a few
    prisoners,
where we shall be pleasant once the future has had its way with us. And you know,
he said, sure, that's the way to hell and its conundrums if that's the way
you want to go, and they all said we know, we are going that way
cautiously approved of in the introduction, only it seems so full of asperities now.
And he said that's the way it was, it was a tangle and will never be anything
more than a diagram pointing you in a senseless direction toward yourself.
Sure, they come with snacks you have foreseen,
but that doesn't excuse you for having been caught in this place. And they all said
giddyap, let's go on to the next
place on the side, for having won, and being here to count up our winnings,
    which are
surely all right with us. Watch it, he said.

So the initial exuberance departed. But that was fine, because surely
the beginning of a festival is a nice place to be, if it's Asia, and more hogs
were brought down. But when he saw the hogs, the owner of the grain elevator
    was angry

and went out. Now, there were two others who were there. And they were
each determined to get what was coming to them. The master returning, said
       OK boys,
never let it be said you didn't ask for it. And in that moment a fuzz of bloom
was on them. Each spring the desert comes alive with birds and flowers,
a breathtaking view at the foot of the famed Superstition Mountains,
reported home of the Lost Dutchman Mine with its still undiscovered caches of gold.
And all around it is nice too. The mineral springs I wanted so much to exploit—what
does any of it matter now, now that I have found my home in a narrow cleft
stained with Indian paintbrush and boar's blood, from which an avenue
       eventually leads
to the flatter, more civilized places I have no quarrel with either. After all,
we *have* to go in once or twice a month to pick up supplies, the few
articles we don't grow such as coffee, to which I'm still addicted by the way, and
records too from a local music shop, which are important to have—no man
needs to live by his own law in the wilderness after all, but even if he is going
to try it is best not to let the old world slip too casually. Rather it should come about
naturally, without too much fuss or horn tooting. And then, by and by, if he sees
he likes it, why then there is always time to make such decisions later on as regards
one's insurance, and such, and peter out from there—trickle accurately
into the sand so that each drop is utilized to the max, and then we'll see
how the desert is improving—only "improve" is a word I don't want to use too much
either. For after all everything is good of its kind to start with. It's all a
question only of finding out what the kind is and letting the thing ferment
in its own bile for a few decades. By then
it should become apparent to whoever has been watching how much the land
       owes us,
and how we re-distribute it wisely, if only we ever stop to think about it. Don't
you agree? I mean, don't you see the silhouetted foothills too? How bland and
       discordant,
yet after all how deeply satisfying in one's rage—and then too the pods fall off

all at once eventually, and must rot
if the seeds are to get into the ground, providing they are still alive and haven't
   rotted too.
So in all ways I think it's a question of a man coming—he had
a chicken or something on his arm. And when he arrived, the expected salutation
rang out like a shot; people took cover. I don't mean
I did, though. I stood up to him, just like a man, the man I was, or is, and he, he just
looked back at me, kind of funny and defiant-like, but he wuz saying nothing.
Too smart for that.

Since the last heist I sense a quintessential weariness; I can
neither lay my barrel down nor look directly into it; I think I'll have a go at the food—
h'mm, squirrel ragout again. No, I'll opt, I'll ope my eyelids for this next one
coming, without food. It was the cutest darn haunted house you ever saw. It had blue
shutters with squirrel cutouts in them. Inside everything was clean and neat.
But haunted houses are like whores—there's no such thing as a nice one, no matter
how prim they act, or how the spotted sun greets them as the warm morning is
   painted.
And then such a one, some other one, would want to know why in the name of
   thunder
these repairs were necessary. After all, the place looked all right. Even the bailiff
who lived next door said so. In the event of a storm or flood, the door
could be shut, and there was an end to it. But it never occurs to anyone that when the
light of the sun does reach the deep pools which are almost always bathed in shadow,
why then a short plop is heard and two people are unable to occupy the same space.
It sounds simple enough in my book. Someone on lead feet looked out
the upstairs window, astonished at the loud knocking below, and then withdrew.
Whether or not this person was actually coming downstairs to answer the door
   was unclear,

at least at first, as minutes and then hours seemed literally to go by. At
midnight the door slowly opened a crack: "Who's there?" Who wants to know?
It would be better if you returned to whatever kingdom you came from. But if
      you sincerely
want to know, bring me boiling water in a paper hat at three minutes before
      two, and that
without spilling a drop. Then I may let you in on my age-old secret, which, of
      course,
isn't mine. I'm only one of a group of seven or eight people who are in on it,
until then.
               I could hear the hissing of soda water in the seltzer bottle and the roar
of the wind in the trees, the cat scratching at the back door, the mice rotating
in place like dust mice, the jangle
of keys the size of fenceposts and the thunk of cylinders as the lock—what was
all the fuss about?—goes through the motions and the clipclopping door falls silent
again. Inside the place reeked of mildew and decay though it looked pretty tidy
considering no one had set foot there for twenty years. A newspaper, still dangling
precariously from the rim of the mail slot, hadn't aged. There was a coffeepot,
      still warm,
on the stove.
               Presently they began the rudimentary preparations for the raindance
everyone knew was to follow in order for the séance to take place. I'll
double you. That's what you think. You can have the two-spot, but please,
leave me the domino with my head scratched into it. Thus the bidding opened,
and it was to be years before it died down again, years that were not unpleasant
on the whole, as many owls stared in amazement at what was happening
      underneath.
What kind of place is this, anyway, to let such things occur in silence?
Surely there must come a time toward the end when an old man gets up
and says what needs to be said? But a rose, or, more precisely, a cactus, could do that
just as well and still leave time for whatever else wanted to get recognized.

§

There is no truth, saith the judge, and one is obliged to concur,
if by truth one means that an occasion has been fitted to an event, and it all came
about just so. If, however, one accepts a broader definition along the lines of
something being more or less appropriate to its time and place, then, by gosh, one is
pretty darn sure of having to own up to the fact that, yes, it does exist
here and there, if only in the gaudy hues of the diaphanous wings
of some passing insect. That is enough, however, to send the scribes back to their
    tablets.
I don't know where this one came in—but wait,
it is of myself I speak, and I do know! But the looks I got convinced me I was
    someone
else as I walked in, not at all sure of myself or (rightly, as it turned out) of
the reception I would be getting. There were framed silhouettes hanging on the walls
of the hall, depicting different forms of mild corporal punishment. A large vase
of pussy willows dominated the sitting room—it was here that the occupants
came to cry, out of vexation or frustration, and whence, having experienced
    some relief,
they departed to seek out others and compare notes
on the battle of time being waged in spiral notebooks and the dour feeling of
banging them shut. There was never any apparent politeness,
but the children sometimes talked with each other for a long time, and, though
conclusions were not ordinarily reached, it shook down some of the stuffing in
    the mattress
of each one's ego, for a time at least. A kettle boiled happily
on the hob. But it was too dark and, above all, too damp to read by. Tall
figures like the shadows of men had been blended into the viscosity of the plastered
walls; in short it was a jungle in there, and though for some reason one
    sometimes felt

tempted to stay, it was obvious that no discussion of the circumstances would ever
be possible. That's when I happened in, wearing a hat, with some sweet breath
of the streets perhaps still clinging to me, and had my say, without being too brusque
about it either, and afterward was shown the tremendous walk-in closets
they build in those climates, those conditions, conditions
which, I want you to understand, aren't all that real. But what's a poor penguin to do?
Meanwhile, fate was simmering down below in its cauldron like some delicious stew
that would never be ready in time; signs of haste in the form of bitten fingernails
and scribbled messages were everywhere apparent, and I have this thing
I must do without knowing what it is or whether anyone
will be helped or offended by it. Should I do it? And there, it was gone.
It will never be printed on a banner in a political demonstration
or fed to rabbits first to see whether they die, and as I live in a house,
am so bound to its principles, in the corners, that coming and going
are very much the same thing to me, in which I no doubt resemble the baby-boomers
who have not let me in peace a single moment since I was thirty years old. Oh,
the good old days! If only we could have received permission to stay a little longer!
But it wasn't to be. So, sadly, I changed into my plain woollen suit
and moved off toward the crest, attitude upgraded. It was a kind of lumber
room, full of boxes filled with papers ("John's report cards") and branches
of artificial holly from Christmases past. It seemed the ghosts
had taken a particular dislike to this room; it felt colder than the others,
though the cold was the result of natural causes. Sunlight, however, warmed the sill.
And I thought of all my lost days and how much more I could have done with them,
if I had known what I was doing. But does one ever? Perhaps it's best
this way, and a riper, more rounded you could only be the product
of so much inefficiency, hence these pear-shaped tones; conversely,
too much planning could have produced a meticulous but dry outline
of what my speech sketches in the rooms, ghost-like, like clouds of steam
on a day of bitter cold, and the minimal progress beyond life's friendly mess
would have meant a severe reckoning and probably an audit

later when it doesn't matter, when only sleep seems of any importance.
At least, that's my reading of it. But what if there were other,
adjacent worlds, at one's very elbow, and one had had the sense to ignore one's
simulacrum and actually wade into the enveloping mirror, the shroud
of a caress, and so end up imbued with common sense but on a slightly higher level,
one step above this one, and then everything you were going to say and
everything they were going to say to you in reply would erupt
in lightning, a steely glitter chasing shadows like a pack
of hounds, once they tasted the flavor of blood, and then this light would gradually
form prickly engraved letters on a page—*but who would read that!*
Who, indeed, would want to know what could have been if one had made the
        slightest
exertion in another direction? So it is always a relief to come back
to the beloved home with its misted windows, its teakettle, its worn places on
        the ceiling,
for better or worse, to the end where battle will be joined
cum frumentum, and heaven commingle in the wide smile of its disheveled
tolerance, and the inspectors, at last, be called in,
though the point was to be done with it without diluting it.
How far does that take you? For the whole
is so pasted over with rags of old posters that only a Bedouin could intuit any rationale,
if then, in its insalubrious confusion. Yet, viewed on another day, there does seem to
be the beginning of a point in how it's boxed in, the hidden partitions
        commenting help-
lessly on what game of linings and the scarcely appreciable removes that make
        them the undersides
this was starting to become. Just as one longs for a solitary hole to call one's own,
so one is horrified at the prospect of being immured in it: that, at any rate,
was my take on the setup this winter. Once past March, the addition
seems not to be complete, to be rambling on to the horizon. So one can lose a
        good idea

by not writing it down, yet by losing it one can have it: it nourishes other asides
it knows nothing of, would not recognize itself in, yet when the negotiations
are terminated, speaks in the acts of that progenitor, and does
recognize itself, is grateful for not having done so earlier.
When all is
demented, no one individual stands out as enormously opinionated. So it goes, and my
goodness, I don't see how we are expected to live with it, but the fact of the matter
is we do and might even consider ourselves improved in respect to the way we were
quite recently, if only we could remember how we looked even this morning, forget
last year or even two or more years ago, so quickly do they pass even in the formal
chronologies and chronicles, I'm
not even talking about the sloppy kind of record-keeping that goes on all the time
without anyone there to be aware of or compliment it.

So seven years passed in whose hollows small, twinkling lights could sometimes
        be perceived
on dark and stormy nights, and the farther one proceeded from one's destination
the closer it seemed and in fact was, though most people took no notice of it
and read newspapers and glanced at swallows exactly as if in Sezession Vienna
        and there
was nothing to think about except one's bowels and the miserable climate.
Breakfasts were consumed; houses were put up for sale; and the whole sad, bad
        shimmer of it
charmed viewers the way a cobra is mesmerized and waves deliciously to and fro
in the temperate breeze, the while sinkholes open up, and K Marts fall into them,
as icebergs are delivered up to the whims of oceans. It wasn't bad while one stood,
but as soon as you sat down you appeared vulnerable; issues were raised; and
        from feeling

it all a mild annoyance but a mere formality, as when a stranger stops you to ask
     directions
and begins asking pointed questions about your religion, it quickly escalated
into a nightmare that waking would not heal. Retreat, retreat! was all they ever
said, and seemed sometimes not to know what they meant. Thus night
appears to have existed always, and to one's surprise one finds oneself
adapting to it as though one had never known anything else, and growing fangs
     and howling
at the moon and avoiding questions from loved ones and overreacting.
Now it was time to be tall too, a further complication. But we were taught that
     everything
is unexpected. Yes, but this is not the moment for recollecting that and even less
to be pondering the reasons for it. Besides we are merely in the middle of it
and can turn our heads to left and right like weathercocks, in deaf amazement
at all that anyone was ever going to do for us and then stopped mentioning.
The orchard that was right for you has stiffened, another autumn is coming
to place its hand across the sun; geese ruffle their feathers and there are
     whitecaps on the pond
and daybreak still eludes us. What could be the point of counting, or counting
     on anything?
The rich *facture* of the trusses and supports is admirable, of course,
knew what it was doing, and burgeoned suddenly, before one had any inkling of it,
drawing alarmed gasps of admiration from the besotted throng. Anyway, it was life,
one had to agree, but all the same could have been better written, with more
     attention
to niceties of style and fewer obscure references, though the concept,
always, was beyond reproach.

§

Wrapped in shawls, was it? And beyond the wharf where sometimes a rope of water
twisted though not for long, the password leading into danger
was "crotchet"—none of us was too sure of what it meant. We knew the reception
we'd get with it, though—a pattern of smiles opening down along the body,
gentle acquiescence to our most childish demands. We came there to be pampered
once in a while, and weren't disappointed. But the lips of the fish, speaking
out of fog, told us another story, which we were bound to recall afterwards
when fires blazed and groups, both sitting and standing, collected around them.
There was this well you looked down into and saw shadows
of bodies caught in trees or washed up on the beach, but the townspeople
never acknowledged anything was amiss: they'd look fixedly at you
if you hinted otherwise, and walk swiftly away muttering something about pearls
or children down there, and how long it takes to really mature anyhow
and who is to be the judge of that? Years later you'd run into one of them at
    a party,
recall what it was, and there'd be only that odd, dank furor of attention,
a glimmer, and then the time frame would change.

In some way the woman knew she was the pivot here, yet it was enough just
being adorable in the sun. A memory of a wish would pass over, but it was a
    bird-shadow,
giving way to frank sunlight the next moment, wholesome in its steady decline
as all things that seek a way out must be—fresh as radishes or Lucerne.
It is time I explained certain tenets of the land
to you, but you see we can never revel in passing back and forth across it:
the understanding has got to be dumb so that others
will think there is a settlement here, and condone development and repairs,
until one day it will be just another paved-over place without sensors:
there is no cause for alarm in this, nor for complacency either, yet it must give way.

Negatively, the posthorn striates the morning gloom since all things have a
    beginning
in something, and it falls back on itself, to material shores, clusters
of formal and market gardens, and there there ought to be an end to it
while the firm old peasant stands, head bowed, cap in hand, but the shrill voices
of children run past him into the near wilderness, and all is scattered again.
My fear is like a small house: you can come visit me
but it will not go away, or will itself into an education; the bonds are loosed,
the pattern lost, and who is to say if I made it up
or someone who was here before and departed, leaving no trace
of his passing, no flicker of ashes in the grate? Or by that time
the note has changed; hereditary enemies greet each other
like long-lost friends; snows melt; the incomprehensible messages
of tree-frogs explicate each other; perspectives, by shifting, have subtly changed
the profiles that stand inside them, and we may not be put to the test
until further legal angles have been explored and resolved, a long way
from here, at some distant point in eternity. Then it will be time
to live off one's resources, but for now one must do battle
with the elements, and stereotypes, and not expect to be called on the carpet
of others' anxious dreams of what is best for us. Go back inside;
it's still chilly out here; the fruit is unripe, and no one knows what time it is.
Pity the seer who gets it right, for he only abideth long,
but at the end is shut out or becomes the toy of others of like condition,
persistent animator. Do, and as I say, so shall the city even
take up the cry and track that one to his lair which is nowhere,
not even eight miles away. The drive, the lunch,
cost more than we knew then, bleary mountain ranges mobilized
against the flight of capital, yet it was hard to see how they could cost more
    even at home
and remain the same, nurse of the arcades to warn the soldiers of potential defeat,
for they came on, blinded by water. The day arrives for him to begin

to grow, but others
in the habitat are puzzled. Wasn't it just such a gentleman, once,
who made the transition from scarecrow to sergeant at arms without anyone's
being the wiser? Has he returned now to sup, yes you too get on with it as you must;
a place is made for him at the table, ere conversation is stilled and a heavy black hand
float above on the wall—no! for if it was my error it was a smallish one, he too
    then beside
us at the deck water pours into. For the one and only is a flower
of the mountaintop and cannot imagine the wrong we have done. They handed
    us over to it
and we were alone.

Soon all the animals acclaimed the victor, still in bed with pilgrims, drunk
with the wine of defeat, and easygoing, like the hero he never had the wisdom
to set out to be. And the line of supplicants led down to some graceless bushes
on fire, for virtue wears many masks. And when it came time to ask him
for the antidote, the dolmens appeared robed in white, and backlit,
and they thought it was an optical illusion. But it was a joke as old as the centipede
at the base of the morass. And seven questioners came, but they too fell to gazing
at the hearty snack he had left untouched, and were troubled. Then before you
    knew it
urchins ran screaming away, it had all been a prank! But some, I believe, were
    convinced,
and to this day swear that a beast had come out of that lair and looked around
and wandered apathetically away, seeing no reason to stay
on and become a weightlifter or *ouvreuse*, but the rest saw it for what it
was, a charade in which they had no part, and began backtracking. And great
    viaducts crashed
of their own accord; supertankers were upended; the cotillion was cancelled

in favor of life-saving exercises, but nobody knew how many, or where the
    implicit tone
or structure was leading. And they turned away stiff-necked. So we were able
to buy a few provisions from the locals, and that is how we got here, and why
we can't stay but a minute, but will see you
on the other side, after the rain, God willing.
And so revived, forgotten, into the long day
angling its shadows at a wider denouement
each time. What would it think of us, if it could think:
mere signers of petitions, names in a long list? Are we tractable
or blotted into the day's fabric like new boys' shouts, the careless exhaust?
Will our pain matter too, and if so, when?

For one pesky minute the wilderness stuck out its tongue
and that was all. Too schooled in its ways to feel adrift for long, I sat
naked and disconsolate at a corner of a crevice, hat in hand, fishing,
for who can tell what God intends for us next? And if a little girl can call
and run, her dog twirl, why not be able to slide a leg over the board
barrier that disconnects us from all that is really happening, that hive
of activity as you think of it? From funky, overexposed moments to plain truths, it is
all there, actually, which isn't to say you desire it yet.
Once the teeth have smiled and the lights been doused yet again, though, it's like
stones caring, and you think, what if that big one up there fell on my head?
Life, read my life, would be over, the jig up, so what's the point
even of moving off somewhere else? Something else could always trigger it.
But I don't want to back off, partly because it isn't
my nature. I think I'll wait behind this old counter, maybe a noise
will remind me a thing isn't right and I'll get
in the groove again. Besides, the wind is a punisher. Tonight

all the old ghosts are back on the radio. How sad that some people have to be
    unhappy
to keep the rest of us barely alive, breathing, I think. I was
in my dressing room and didn't hear it. It must have gone through the house
    like a bird's swoop
yet I am innocent, my clothes, the ones I've hardly worn, barely on.
Now the official announcement, probably. These dustcatchers . . . Look, if you're
    going to swear
you may as well leave, you can come with me, I'm leaving this place.
I've had it. Twenty centuries is too much. Just drifting, like a leaf, is more
than I bargained for, at the beginning when the tin was new, the smoke clean, and
a bramble's red could scorch your heart, leaving you alone, and now it's too late
for pie and others. All's stranded. The pergola in the plaza beckons
still but it's the smile
of a latecomer, all candy and cigarettes, no more insulation for the cheers and
    puffery
we assumed would be forthcoming until he sets down his tray and it was empty
except for a dirty napkin and an orange stick; whose business are you playing
with now, in front of the old microphone? Painted
a bit more lugubriously now, true, but the busboys, the brunch crowd want
    danger; zero in
on sloth; what's a poor old fright to do? Suicide? No, I don't think you . . .

It was then I discovered the pavements were made of the same flagstones found
    underseas
except there they were arranged more brightly in schools; here, clusters
are the thing. School is for kids. I think I'll go, Miss MacGregor, honest
I will, this time or bust? You have cleared out my lounge . . .

There is no place to talk, no amphitheater
under which we can put our heads, deducing all-too-violent theorems, yet
I quite like it, one is active. Besides, didn't I hear you say our daddy was once
     picked up
here by the secret police, and shaved heads are no longer the thing inside the gates,
and the stand of birch is there, but it is all, there is nothing left over
to eat a sandwich next to? If he had tried too soon, if the sun . . . But plus or minus
is unimportant; beware of negative thoughts. The ewe and the prunes are mine
anyway; insistence on finer points is the stuff highwaymen's dreams are made
     on, until
the lost chord; it sounded so brittle back there. Come to my desk, we'll talk it out
and by George the next time it will come round, in a dress, and we'll all thank our
premonitions and the power of staying up alone
in a rain-lashed stadium with the TV on. So much power, at such a distance.
     But it glows.

All along I had known what buttons to press, but don't
you see, I had to experiment, not that my life depended on it,
but as a corrective to taking the train to find out where it wanted to go.
Then when I did that anyway, I was not so much charmed as horrified
by the construction put upon it by even some quite close friends,
some of whom accused me of being the "leopard man" who had been terrorizing
the community by making howl-like sounds at night, out of earshot
of the dance floor. Others, recognizing my disinterest, nonetheless accused
me of playing mind-games that only the skilled
should ever attempt. My reply, then as always, was that ignorance
of the law, far from being no excuse, is the law, and we'll see who rakes in
the chips come Judgment Day. I can see why someone who didn't know me

might be kind of appalled at this flip attitude, but was unprepared for the chorus
of condemnatory shrieks from the entourage, as though *they* hadn't been through
much of it themselves, and could cast the first stone. Once upon a time,
however, I was new to it and felt the land catching up to me
as on the outskirts of a town where one is seeking a night's lodging
unprepared for whatever consequences may befall. I spent a week once
in someone's house in a small town in Pennsylvania, without ever
learning whose it was, or addressing anyone by name. Another time, in Maine,
I found myself face to face with a wolf at sunset. So you see, my
rationale is that I've taken my lumps as well as enjoyed the good times
now and then, and don't see what difference it makes to old soldiers,
of which I'm proud to count myself one. On at least one occasion
when I felt I hadn't slaked the lime sufficiently, so to speak, it all seemed
to be going from bad to worse. I had my companions, and my kit,
and was ready to pack it in as soon as morning arrived, glad
to escape with my skin intact. But then a curious thing happens:
an old guy comes up to you and tells you, reading your mind, what a magnificent
job you've done, chipping away at the noble experiment, and then, abruptly,
you change your plans, backtrack, cancel the rest of the trip
that was going to promise so much good health and diversion for you; you suddenly
see yourself as others see you, and it's not such a pretty sight either, but at
least you know now, and can do something to repair the damage, perhaps by
looking deeper into the mirror, more thoroughly
to evaluate the pros and cons of your success and smilingly refuse all
offers of assistance, which would be the wrong kind anyway, no doubt, and set out
on your own at the eleventh hour, into the vast yawn or cusp that sits
always next door. And when we have succeeded, not know what to do with it
except break it into shards that get more ravishing as you keep pounding them. See,
I am now responsible though I didn't make it. And you
can come back, I'm harmless now. Anyway, that's how it pleases me to
detect myself. When the blossoms reappear, as they can, and the consumers,

someone must pay to keep it poignant. Otherwise one of you will remain an
    outrider.
Go finance the rigged deal then, and it can't hurt.

It worked. Now both of us were attracted.

Let me by way of introduction hopefully
try to extricate myself from this peculiar bunch of circumstances,
the slough. Incidentally I am a gentleman
for some of my dealings. Nor do I believe in one set of laws for the rich,
another for the poor, nor in one thing over another, one mother-in-law,
one pasture for ducks, another for swans. Permit me to posit,
though, another way of looking at the situation, awful now,
as it has been in the past when they had less hygiene but more spirit of things
than is alas now the case. What if you let everything bounce off you except those
things whose nature it is to imbed themselves in you? Like a sharpened pencil
    forever
flailing the dark with one's own tangles, one nears an edge. There are two
    possibilities:
ignore it or cross it anyway. In either case we'll be
rid of our relatives' nosiness and can get down to business quite quickly. I say "I"
because I'm the experimental model of which mankind is still dreaming, though
    to myself
I'm full of unworked-out bugs and stagefright, yet manfully I put aside those
    twenty years
to imagine some croft or bourne in which a few of us can weep, as flute-notes play,
and others can come round nodding approval and must then be on their way.

But—by heaven!—I think we almost knew just then what it meant to be together
without too many people around, how it could challenge the universe's bluster,
the hee-hawing ages in the time it takes to put an idea together
from its unlikely components, package it, and go on being the genius one was
    anyway
but not for too long, or without general consent. It's enough if—
my friend's mother is the one who believes in me and understands me better
than anybody, but I'm not going to let it delude me. There's a world out there.
So, drunk, we come back to the dollhouse open to the elements,
its scuffed paper furniture, to try to feed on newsprint once more,
unsuccessfully. But the old lady wants to explain what happened, indeed
there's no way to ignore her account of what happened, so let's just
sit still and listen. This, according to her, is what did:

slippery harmonies abound. In fact, I can't be sure I'm not addressing myself
to one or within one right now, but that's no matter. I've got to tell this
in whatever time remains to me. You and I were young, at lunch, we jumped up
in that mad way one has of wanting to see how things will react, wanting to see them
turn out, as it were—an ancient, though harmless, temptation. Wait, there was more:
after the gentleman had gone, leaving me his card, I stood in the hall
for a long time, unable to go back to the kitchen or up the stairs
I knew so well. I reflected on all the ways we have of quietly
getting each other's goat, of stewing over inconsequential things. The morning
had passed without event, and now, on the threshold of afternoon, I could lean out
into the bowl of eternity, like a poster
plastered to the wall of a house, advertising a brand of cigars, as the future
came dripping back with intent, impregnating me like a wick with its
    contradictory

or spurious commands, futile innuendo, explosions of choices before one is ready
to choose, like team-colors. And as I stood, contemplating the card, sinking
into the primness of outline for which I seemed to have turned into a walking or
at any rate standing testimonial, and the years mounted the wick, I see I am as ever
a terminus of sorts, that is, lots of people arrive in me and switch directions but no one
moves on any farther; this being, in effect, the end of the line, a branch-line
at that, and no one is interested in guessing, in passing through you
or fancying they spy more copious rewards you are presumably keeping them
    from accepting,
once they have come of age. True, a few dawdlers will move on briskly, then turn
back officiously to salute you, as though polite gestures could dilute the heavy
water of eternity, or what's left of it, which, it is naturally assumed, is inferior
to what has gone before—and then manage to insult your prudence by ignoring it
on this windblown platform you share with pigeons, not even
another bona fide passenger. And one's dream of escaping weighs on your
shoulders, like a yoke of steel. Could one even contemplate it
now? Now that so many other things and soldiers are coming to be
what must be, and in fact has always been? A towering tree? But, speechless,
we make it over into miniatures of itself, like miniature automobiles. Then
a perfectly sweet, sickly stench bears this notion over to the main table,
numbers it, sets it down with the others, while the concept of an alphabet can
still be sustained (but the curtain is falling on that particular misunderstanding,
    and on
much else as well, including some factors I would like to conserve in the new,
stripped-down, presumably more functional civilization the alphabet-wand
seemed to want to announce), walks hurriedly out of the great *gare*, without
so much as a backward glance, into a post-Wagnerian, impressionist world of rivers
and dreaming washerwomen, and stones at the edge. Well, whose maelstrom
was it, and what are you talking about? I think to see a bulb blooming; a little mote
in the sunlight, if that's it, would be fine for this morning. (Oh, you do,

do you?) And afterwards shut up about it. It's in the mail anyway.
A fine thing that nobody talks to me or his parents. How am I supposed to know which
ticket goes with which entrance portal? *And the woman with orange-pink hair stood silently by.*
And, not knowing, to whose parents am I to address the grievance form?
Believe that a change infuses the young, though they aren't enthusiastic.
For it is not a shifting of gears nor a vrooming of motors that is the note
one hungers after, but just as the distracted dripping of a stalactite produces,
in the fullness of time, a perfectly viable stalagmite, so one's fretting and anxious
reverberations are but the negative space that gives birth to this invisible but densely
compacted mass of fibers that filter truth: the Last Judgment (text enclosed).
Paganini on his cloud fiddles; lambs gambol; appealing nonsense would seem to have
had the last word again. Yet when you see from a great distance how it forms a
pattern, then other conditions have to be taken into account, their probability admitted
into the record, a court order produced putting it all on hold and speedily overruled as the
dynamics gets into your blood and you find you can live without it. Yes, but
meaningfully? No, the hold order is still in effect, though it was supposed
to have been lifted; the tape is blank. But I thought those were
unimportant details somebody else was supposed to see about? Sure they were
but time is up now, and the pugilists have returned to their corners. Write about it,
if you were going to be interested in it, right now, if not
otherwise involved with its destiny. It's the old "elaborate charade" accusation
again, and I'm not going to have any truck with it, or with you either. I don't
know how many times I've spelled the B-word accurately without being credited,
so in the time of doppelgangers I be a lost bairn—without spelling, I mean,
though I used to do well in the spelling bees.

                    Which reminds me,

how are Alf and Al? Did I leave anything out? Does the lagoon
still stink? Or did somebody drain it after all those years of miasma
and not-too-amusing going about one's business, sometimes
with a handshake or a smile?

But if one's destiny is enclosed in one's brain, or brain pan, how about free will
and predestination, to say nothing of self-determination? Just how do they
fit together? I know I explained this once but
that was a cold while ago and now this upstart rephrasing of it seems to be
causing a lot of attention, I don't know why. It's only a re-working, a scissors-
    and-paste
job; the wording is almost identical, and still there are some benighted souls
who follow it, day by day in its lumbering, tumbrel-like progress across edifices,
burial sites, unnamed and unnamable sumps, for all the world
to see in its glory, for all the world as though something were emerging
and they were going to a circus or a party. Too bad the old people couldn't have
known about it before it was actually announced. Some of the young too were
tempted to skip until I stepped down from my soap-box to have a go at lecturing
    them
in real earnest, though with a joke or two added as leavening, or gilding the
pill as you might say. For if they had known first
they wouldn't have minded not knowing after it had all happened, in vain,
one supposes, again. It's too bad there aren't more students
or even a few customers. The weather and the rushes scare tourists away
and waste sets in. The season is spectacular. Here, take my viola
da gamba, that dump again, it had a . . . Sipping ouzo is something.
But in all the thirty-nine territorial states drains are backing up;
for the first time something like resentment is making itself felt
in the trees, on the lawns. It's still possible to chat with one's neighbor over

the back fence, but the quality of life has been imperceptibly diminished
by too much arguing over the status of life today—that is, how is it felt subtly
in one's veins, how does it differ from before, how is it that one day we think we see it
and the next day it seems gone, gone forever? Yet we do go on living—how does
that work? In the next field, a farmer is driving a rig of some kind—who is
expected to pay for the difference between what he sees up close and what is in
    the skies
now, with better labeling? More importantly, are they gone, the old familiar faces?
In time living on into a new share of English promise, some of
the junior ones went over the wall, and that was the last we saw of *them*.

Still, it's a chance. One can easily side with some who offer no
moral incentive to cling together, who are, in their own words, "racked up,"
meaning blighted, for as long as cosmopolitan history chooses to entertain them,
    and no
offense either. That is, some are neanderthal diehards, you always get a few, but in
a notable number of instances there is no or not much prejudice; the eyes, wiped clean,
are ready for the prepared statement as it sings in the street like a serpent.
There isn't much you can do, and it's
a little darker. Tell it the time. And on no account lose your bearings
unless you want to wash up like a piece of polyester at the gulf's
festering edge. That tanker took on more water. The consensus was there *would* be a
symposium, if anyone could be found to host it. Meanwhile things are getting
    a little better
on that front too, which includes romance. It too
is highly nutritious. Homey. Just in time for some fun, pranks, feelings; it may
be time to get off now, to swap it for a bigger parcel, trade up
to new ruthless schoolroom dreams while keeping the coded receipt just in case
we may make another big slip and water cannot satisfy competing demands.

We'll still have an area with water, but like I say, juvenile bombast and
       highjinks bid fair
to drown out the other uproar, domesticate it and pass it on to their offspring
in Rome, where the dahlias blow, and sweet crocuses and cats by the score as the
       spring
billboard begins again. But *durch ein ander*. Smell it yourself he said my gosh.

And admit of sexual practices? Proclivities? The right to kill and maim? I suppose . . .
Night was floral at that post. It was fashionable to throw out last year's buggery
along with the rented skis, and hope no one saw you. Besides, what could be said
about those mosaics? That they looked on, wore down, smooth as old storks' nests,
witnesses to so much casual butchery, that a stringy music rose out of it
to command our measured pace back into history and then see it alive, tobacco- and
offal-stained, till we knew not who we were but only what we had to do.

The thunder could be heard all over the city.
Sometimes it is taken to extremes; the "extreme mind" thinks it can
understand what it means to it. The peculiar magic
of our idiom so enchanted her, with the vacuum of each thought,
that it even seemed permissible to escape around the edges and start running away,
though that is another story. What matters to us is that an unstable air
of permissiveness was in the streets, close, like a thick mist
or mitt, on the tongue, leading in some instances to crushes.
Little was ever made of the anomaly that we grew up here; indeed
it was never factored into the partial account that we succeeded only after
many demands in having read aloud, in a halting tone, next to a fountain, so
       that the tumbling

of pebbles obscured our larger words, in some cases replicating them in miniature,
obsequious to a fault. The ham-handed rendition made a botch of the layers
of meaning and the layers of bread, satisfying neither reporters nor hierophants.
We all returned home anxious
to get the night over with.

And end it did, yet scarcely
in the ways one had imagined, but with a finality as
inexplicable as its itinerant birth some years back down the creek. First,
there was a lot of hammering. Then a blonde woman got out of the car to take
      pictures.
H'mm, this must be *the* night, a lot of people mistakenly assumed. Then the thunder
again—I can't possibly tell you what was in it for me, so rounded
were its periods, like an architecture erupting from the earth;
like a repertory of trees, from which emerged cries,
or so it seemed. That these were the damned of the earth
in whose look colorful arcs beat the meaning down
to size, proud of being duly noted, was acknowledged by no one of rank.
Feathers first, then dust, then flourishes
in a signature, with the bad taste to insist on the letter of personality lessons
taken at some charm school in hell, were the note struck, and that you
were a few years older than me, and that sufficed to bring the argument
to a graceful dead-end near where the coats were. Yet sometimes in the quietism
I miss your cracked precision, knowing it could have taken us this far
in the storm's well-oiled chariot without making a production number
of it and we should have been well equally, only now
what does it matter? I mean, whose shortcomings are we talking about,
except it's better to go over at the last
moment and make your peace, whatever that can be.

§

There was something I liked in the way of beginning
and something also in the way of returning, though it made us sad.
Next spree though, try to find us a different decade: this one's already full.
The twaddle dispensary's reopened. The French still say "hailstones big as pigeon's
eggs," and poets are retreating into—or is it out of?—academia, beset by the
usual pit-bulls and well-meaning little old ladies in tennis shoes. And discovering
and assimilating new bastions of indifference and comprehension. What else?
That was some storm we had last week. The webs intersect at certain points
        where baubles
are glued to them; readers think this is nice. What else? Oh, stop badgering—
where were *you* in the fifties?

Indeed. Alvin and the chipmunks made nice ambient music for what
I was fussing over, or masticating, and I had to find a way out of the woods.
Now, in some cases, this is easy—you just walk straight along a road and pretty soon
you're out of the woods and there are suburban backlots. In my case,
though, it wasn't that simple, though it wasn't extraordinarily demanding either—I
just lay down in a boat and slept, Lady-of-Shalott style. Soon I was gliding among you,
taking notes on your conversations and otherwise making a pest of myself.
I pretended to be angry when onlookers jeered and cows mooed and even the
        heralds told me to shut up,
yet at bottom I was indifferent. I knew my oracles
for what they were—right about 50% of the time—and I also knew their
        accuracy wasn't
an issue. It was the repeating of them that interested me. Repetition makes reputation.
Besides, it's something you can build with. You need no longer inspect the materials

when you buy them in bulk; they are as a territory. What gets built happens
to be in that territory, though beside it. Your reputation as a builder
is the one interesting thing.

In the sixties new dresses were newer.
The humbler children were clad in dimity, and bird-cheerful. Airlines seldom
overbooked. My imagination was trying to get its act together, I mean really see
itself. But like the site of Carthage, which was circumscribed by strips of some
animal's hide, it could not really accept itself for all it was because of the
possibility that a trick was involved. And yet, shaking its hair
and staring at its crystal reflection in some drop of dew, it also knew it wasn't
nothing, and something had to account for this. I think the constant costume changes
caused it to mistrust itself, yet there was a game to be played, and rules to abide by—
so what? It's true in other walks of life . . . But it all led rapidly to the crunch
of where the fuck do you think you're going? *This* is the frontier.
Beyond lies civility, a paradise of choices—maybe. But it wasn't made to be tested
by such primitive assaying tools as you, and only you, come equipped with.

I saw your face on some bookjacket. It looked beautiful. May I write to you?
I wouldn't really swallow poison if I was you. Meanwhile I have the rain
to experience with the others, each of us finding it uncomfortable though seldom
talking about it, as there are more important subjects. Fishing, for example.
I have to get home before the music disappears. I love you.
I thought I said never to come in this café?

Finally all will survive because of fierce determination. I mean,
they're tough, people are. Hey guys,
what accounts for losses along the way? The house is built,

the beds made, and see how it comes undone, but then an enormous ray of sunlight,
like a minor flood, imbues the room, and once again we are saved from ourselves
as something rings down the curtain on us gloriously. One lived principally by
       one's wits
and therefore was not surprised by this sudden reversal: it always has something
of us in it, so I signed it. It wasn't long in coming, but was just my hope,
ironed and carefully hung on a hanger in a closet, and it was endearing, but that
       wasn't
why I loved it. All loves are quite pleasant, and this one, being for myself,
was especially so. Now that so much has simply dropped out of life, more
than one can take the pulse of, one isn't sure, in this rout, this retreat
from a great city, how much of it is left in there. It seems only yesterday
that one could find cheap walkup apartments in the East 50s, and modest restaurants
such as the Cloisters, with $1.95 complete lunches, or luncheons. When was the last
time you had luncheon? The atmosphere was thinner, but more abundant, and
       well worth
the few extra cents. Besides, I had begun working on something like
my autobiography, I was going to distill whatever happened to me, not taking
       into account
the terrific things that didn't, which were the vast majority, and maybe if I reduced it
all sufficiently, somebody would find it worth his while, i.e., exemplary. And
       then in the rush
to evacuate I left the precious notebook behind; there simply wasn't time to look
       for it;
but I could have reconstructed it, drop by drop, from what I remembered, having
kept close watch over what went in, yet this would in some way have falsified
everything, one of the points being that one makes a show of what one rejects,
the better to flaunt what one enshrines, but that
can only happen once in the way of things happening. Yet that was more than a
       generation ago,
or more, depending on how you define a generation now. What are you saving it for?

And a horn screeched. Particles turn nasty. The other
is there, besides. We cannot move. The fullness in the house at night
is only a diagram (but cling to it, anyway) of where things were, and though
we can remember what things, they are gone now; only their relation
to one another subsists, and I am as a dog. It seems I can't think. I remember
      once under trees
receiving the warm but peculiar and complicated presence, like Leda her swan;
I smiled convulsively and in an instant was left
somehow darkened, though the pressure
was relieved and since then has never been a problem. But I, as the other (as I now
see myself to have been), was no wiser and certainly no better
for the terrible irruption into my life. It has made everything I've said since
sound silly, yet I won't debate the point, which after all is
nothing more than that a light, and some warmth, stood in my life for five
      minutes once
and ever afterward has remained unto me, though I often
forget it for decades at a time, yet am forgiven
when it turns up again, like a smile. These seem like facts
to me; no politics attaches to it; yet in the stalemate of centuries it could
turn once to me and utter my name. That's all I ask. I'd be forgiven
then, and focus my energies on something more important like rebuilding our wall,
expecting nothing in return but the verdict, and then I'd go down
into the vicarious city expecting nothing but vibrations, the verdict: the one
you always said you couldn't stay to see me get, it would be too confusing
and painful to our house, too unexpected: inexcusable. (That word.)

Last night you weren't so sure. And it goes on:
There was once a shopping mall
at my place. Kids went to it. Mottled houseplants were sold to alert

home-makers, in that light. You could buy quantities of them
and leave them in your yard. Or mix them with others; try to get the most out of
the variety, as it sifts down to you: the great speckled hen
on the lookout, or the hyena I dreamed of last night, or salmon leaping in their beds:
all are abrupt elements in the sum listening leads to, cannot renege on
unless *you* backtrack, become the slightly less valuable person of a few minutes ago
with the feathered headdress and baubles. That one. But the sum will get lost
    anyway
in the crowd, unless drastic measures are taken. And who is to take them?
Because you, walking around comparison-shopping, are its infrastructure
and the only one who will bring it to the edge of a cross-section of the people's
    imaginings.
See, there might be already a little canopy over the pier
but more likely not; it's still early in the season; the river's rank winter smell
still pierces the air's musky crevices; the grass isn't right and
there's too much pre-freshness. The real thing won't be around
for days, even weeks. And we're supposed to get on with the project, somehow,
settle down in the logic these lines always left space for, between them, but which
was rarely visited by any save sandwich men and vagrants, more's the pity when
    you see how
idle folk get well off and we stand hands clasped to breasts still worrying about the
back taxes that were never paid one year, because this isn't forgotten by anybody
but becomes one of those rust-colored lots thieves and innocent children hang out in,
like the one where Mercury slew Argus for vulgar reasons,
reasons of his own imagining. Now that the moon's up
they say there won't be any rutabagas
till next year. But go on, I have to go out and fight
about it with everybody, even my superiors
in my place of employment
which is dry and casually tidy as the next person's. Only I do so out of a great fear
the man I entered may not be enough, may thoughtlessly

send me back to the end of the line that meanders
from here to the desolate, reedy horizon. What did I ever do to resent you, open
    your calm
caresses like oysters? And then is it right to save them? Might I be
reading a magazine when it all happens to me, this time, and now I stand up
baffled by the sandstorm, because how did I know it was zeroing to this
ungainly end, not see any danger signs, not shut off the hose, though I am gifted
with a suit of eyes and can foretell the near future and recall the recent past? Is it
that I'm a sort of jerk?
                    No, oceans were hiding, waiting
on your bald spot; pencils with chewed points told us all we'd need to know
until the twenty-first century, whereupon we'd all come out of our lairs, mew
and make up. And now that doesn't seem such a good idea, that stronghold
has got to last. Otherwise midnight and the fires
jabbering, like we were taught, will ruin all chances of an application
before it's forwarded. And stones come down from trees. No kidding it's a splendid
series; no way would you want to miss out on it. I have to grow though.
I must go back in time. It's not the way you heard it
in the alley or over the transom. For though hard work is indeed
a key ingredient, no one can know the outcome until all are banished by ill will
or saved and the mongrel idiot takes the credit for it
and then sleeps, it too, for the path is what you call freckled with blemishes.
No ape nor man stands alone who knows it,
who can recite it backwards. In the orchard, and that's the least
of my worries. I have to put you on hold again.

But what do we know? We're not authentic crime-busters,
only pals of the accused from school. When he wrote those
seemingly contradictory rules, he never dreamed we'd end up

following them, and him, into the oblivion he decreed for us.
Now it all seems an antique space in which they talked
much as we do, feared God, forgave
each other the endless trouble someone was always causing—not that
it wasn't justified in some instances by the confusion of late spring and early summer.
We heard each case. Then, if punishment was in order it was meted out
impartially and the whole business quickly forgotten, in the interests
of the children. Wait, there were arguments on both sides—
but it seems as though a stormy prelude had gotten out of hand; suddenly
everyone was running. But you know what I mean. They were like super-gullible
and had to be made to understand, even through tears, thrashings, moans.
Then I like the idea of coming out at the top
for a brief time to survey what's happened down below
and retreat, the better to tidy up loose ends, weave reports
around this affair that brought us so much ridicule, so much deserved
attention. Besides, the plaster arches had taken on an air of permanence
long ago and were in danger of being confused with the real thing; one had to
shuffle the cards, put a brave face on it; otherwise we ourselves might have ended up
imagining we stood at the apogee of empire and power and forgotten to go in at night
or take temporary precautions. Then when the collapse finally maneuvered itself
into being we'd have no one to blame but ourselves, and be forced back
into a primary mood of spells and rituals. You didn't want that. That's how we
ended up winning, which is another story. Had we
however mistaken the early chirpings for pre-emptive strikes there's a good
    chance we
might have ended up contemplating the sky from the other side, its stickers and
    warnings
looking interchangeable thanks to the tame minority decisions we'd endorsed,
never having run up against any precedents for dealing with superannuated, frayed
systems until they'd been polished to look like the present and were therefore
of no use to us or to anyone else either. How far we'd

strayed from the bend in the stream, but the current
seemed to push us forward, whispering words of encouragement, and the
    poplars laughed
and danced and smiled seemingly at us, but that was a pathetic fallacy,
of course. They never saw us. Not even once. Not us.

Quick—the medication. But the house had no sense at all, and having
become a limited partner in my own disestablishment, I watched in terror
as it moved on us, dull plumage of another kind,
condensed around doors and windows, with a sense of authority
still, like a wishbone in the throat, the docket
whose very plainness might be
adjudged a virtue. What is this? A frigid sense
of isolation, tarnished beyond knowledge? Yes, and the others tell
it differently, and their version too is the truth, or it is truthful.
And many of these were going up
into the house where he watched the city, and then
these others were below, but they did not matter so much. I was basking
on my sunlit shelf, like a tomato plant. *That* mattered. And the fact that there
    were so many
more speaking rationally mattered. And they began to scream, shrieking things like
where were you born, who got you started anyway? And in truth
I fumbled the question now, and the answer came from all over, randomly inclusive.
A ruthless teen dissolves equations you can't bear to look at
before it's all over but the shouting, and others prod
the old trunk, wanting some credit, like graffiti artists, shouting too.
I thought I was immune to it, having been stung once,
but I'm not. And I ask you, in the name of all that's reasonable . . .

§

Others were shot. As I see it the main difficulty is getting used
to the gradual increase in light increments, walking home in the early evening
after a day at the office, and being back
in the apartment again, if only for the night.

And the mounting green. Each year, spring is more powerful,
gaps in its front are fewer, sizable runs on the arsenal at the observatory more
        remarked.
And the truth sits rigid. What does it have to contribute after all?
No charm, certainly. And precious little of the bread one weeps eating
having taken the cross, and all else is "nice" or "interesting" in that lurch
before one sees. Truly sees, that is when it is too late
even for memories and rumors, the starched ballgown, the paymaster's slips,
and when it's too late, it's too good too. Otherwise they'd follow us
into this dawn, ask us misleading questions, like liars. Well,
some of us have to be. We'd see about that. "Anon." I asked about the witches' society
but you'll have to grovel, to find out where they put it, where they're
off to next, unless a lucky blight disclose as a side-effect the thrust
of its situation we're leading down to. Yes, the harvest home had no walls at all.
And I got off at the corner. I hear America snowing. I want it to
confront me, not my fate, with the possibilities of the next change, but we
        pretend there are
reasons not to blur the wall between them and us, not to step down,
and become one in a group of opportunists like ourselves, and so matter peculiarly
before tomorrow's decision, the battle of compromise. Yes, and you took over.

§

Not that I think for a moment that . . . And grasping that quiddity like an ox's
     neck, without
warning he came at me. Relentlessly the minutes, some of them golden, touched.
His task force inserted itself. It was almost lazy how the spars of flame floated
down, and continued to burn on the grass, but this was a kind
of joke, a celebration. The hundred-year-old ivy marked the ridges on the tegument
where nodules of revolutionary thought were beginning to form, and splinter,
     leaving
the dark, obdurate mass of negative energy, confined in a ball, to point to
having its day in the near future—quite soon, mind you—and bill collectors
in an outer room. Reading, apparently. Then a wolf-moan, in guise of roll-call,
blew up the ammunition dump. There were artificial legs everywhere
and kindly geezers standing under umbrellas, softly asking things
like where is the next scrunched-up ball of paper and can my daughter-in-law,
     who lives
alone, touch any benefits from the sick behemoth's collapse, who was
never particularly outgoing in his day but now wants to be part of the birthday
     celebration
just as kings and princes do. And with that on my mind, I searched the grass
for signs of the coming progress. And they all went back into their houses
and that was all for that day.

But I am prepared now for the drone that submerges grace-notes in the conviction
of its being. To listen only for a moment is to bathe
in it as in a possibility—the first one—and you can shut your ears anyway
from the tirade in its later stages, assuming one wants to

not get off until the sudden unnatural brightness that indicates the last stage of the
voyage has been inaugurated, that we're in for some fun and enlightenment
now which takes the form of bad dreams—you know that one you're terrified of
    having
again, and it always turns out to be rather nice
at the end? Besides, a delegation of schoolchildren has come to thank you for it,
for having it, and thus allowing yet another generation to grow up unmenaced
by the plans of bureaucrats for civilization a few years down the pike, every year
or so. You see it is part of your plan, gestates with you,
because of you, and in you—never mind that it's too shrill for some ears to pick up
on, that's what protects us during the periods of ritual slump and restores
some of one's original dignity like a lost lace christening-robe—besides,
they weren't very fat in those days, or somebody had to wear those things.
There were governesses and servants then, which seems almost magical now, almost
beyond belief. Simple lives were also led. In short the world was a great
circus ring in which one could witness proud doings and glimpse one's fellow
spectators on the opposite side, and everything turned to song like fire, hustled
into the furnace of energetic living, and the sad birds
walked away, were seen no more. Thus evening
when it arrived took on an orgiastic purity that was understood as of a piece
with the fabric, dim and buried in spray as it might have appeared
sometimes, until the truth will out, and vociferousness have its day, as is
only right, and we should think about it, and come back to it sometimes, at
    other times.

I now find it deeper, though quieter, to prepare this
and have come belatedly to realize that sex has very little to do with any of it,
that is directly, except insofar as it makes you do something you hadn't thought about
because it brought you to a place you hadn't thought of visiting,

some quiet corner of a garden, unnoticed before, whose perfection of design
no longer now seems a threat, but rather a greeting instead.
I was hurrying on my way as usual, too bored to notice the look of calm self-esteem
of those who circulated near me, nor give back what I had accepted as readily
as a drop of rain, token of the neutral benevolence that waits and pours
at certain corners where the road is taken up again
like a shuttle. There will always be someone to share the burden; even
oxen are true, as under burnished leaves they sidle
forth at morning, or return at evening without much commotion, without
making too much of it. And our dreams are scanned and dissolved in these
    seemingly
pointless rituals (unless the point is to release us as they smash the perfect design,
for mere symmetry is death, and their rounds would be that if shattered wreaths
didn't loom in the wake of their indifferent passage). But there I go,
attributing impartial goodness to the coils of superstitious industriousness that
    shored
me for a moment and let me down easy: bunches of grapes
the fox didn't even bother to shrug at, passing into the golden dust-clouds,
the clank of arms and clumsy restitutions, of that middle distance
where old man and girl alike play, and the shadow can never creep near enough
to explode the myth of the day we have, the scale to be played.

No matter that it didn't make me look ridiculous—the point is I could easily
    have managed
that without assists from bunnies and wood-sprites if something not of my own
    construing,
something I rejected, hadn't interposed a feline quickness and fur just before the fatal
gradient, and I stepped back and stared, and in that moment saw myself on a
    visit to myself,

with quite a few me's on a road receding sharply into a distance spiked with blue
fantastic crags that had castles perched on them and were honeycombed with
    grottoes. I could as easily
have missed it and arrived blind at my destination, this room
where I entertain a stranger as dusk deepens and silence settles in,
and never known my own two shoes, what to make of them,
as they scoured hills as well as dales in search of the person they
belonged to instead of staying parked under this plain wooden table.
Something else will break fruitfully
the allotted chain of associations, and it will serve as well—only don't try to pass
    it off as
an impulse, sincerity. Too much of the city remains standing for that
and the canker must burn in the memory, red as loganberries, for the lever
to cancel the fulcrum, for a new age of nothing to come into being,
attracting as little attention as possible,
that all may live
to do justice to the gods that set us in motion! Hesperides!

Any day now you must start to dwell in it,
the poetry, and for this, grave preparations must be made, the walks of sand
raked, the rubble wall picked clean of dead vine stems, but what
if poetry were something else entirely, not this purple weather
with the eye of a god attached, that sees
inward and outward? What if it were only a small, other way of living,
like being in the wind? or letting the various settling sounds we hear now
rest and record the effort any creature has to put forth to summon its spirits
    for a moment and then
fall silent, hoping that enough has happened? Sometimes we do perceive it
this way, like animals that will get up and move somewhere and then drop down

in place again, we hear it and especially we see it—some whitecap curdles
in a leaden expanse of water and we are aware this moment
has done its share, that we shall not be needing this batch of insight again.
Yet other times it all comes stampeding into the foreground, crushing one's toes,
       a question
like the question of what to wear, and then we fall back, confused, we know we
       are not
smart enough, that we can never anticipate all the trials that will have been
       administered
just now, forget those to come when we and our kind have been forgotten
in some memorial dump of time, with stone lotuses and iron epaulets, and they
       called you
a wheeler and dealer, and yes that is what fate reserves for the most capable,
even; they called you a leader and here you are, with us in the kingdom of
       ghosts; only don't
tarry too long with your inaugural address: others are waiting to mount the lectern.

Yet there are other times as in a quarry where no breeze stirs; nothing
indicates it; poetry scarcely drips from vines, the weather is hugely oppressive, yet
you do know something is at work in you, something else: take death away and still
a vast alteration remains to be made. We know this decade doesn't fit,
that we can do nothing about it except swear, yet it *will* do, it will have to. A fly
dies, and then? Who are we to speculate on the delicious paradoxes that will
       outlive us,
embroiled in street things, squeezing a pimple until some richly satisfying
pus comes out? Were we needed then?
                              Almost casually, gigantic cardboard cutouts
of mammoths and hydras appear in the wings, and one knows, not having done
       one's homework,

that the spells will materialize as dots joined together, and the casual
whirlwind that vaporizes moods and intensity of expression was an astrologer's error;
here, it sits on a doorstep, waiting for the "back in five minutes" tenant to materialize
with all the lawsuits and indecent percentages in its wake, but that's no matter,
it's a river and one must keep up with it.

Another time I was just sitting, on a rung.
Some kids were playing ball. I asked what it meant that we
never did anything, were content to let others do things and play,
as though it were for us. He said, sure thing. I said I'd had a nap,
what I wanted now more than anything was that someone would come and play
         with me;
I'd then decide whether to or not. She said, but this is all some kind of love ambush.
The boys don't play with you, they have to play with themselves. You're
         supposed to find some
kind of message in it, when the weather takes you away for a day
and delivers you back home, as though from a fishing trip, and no one can say
you are any different, or notice a different twinkle in the eye. But it is all changed
even though you and they would prefer not to admit it.
You're a grown man now, but must sit in a tub. I agreed that it was so,
but said I'd always imagined that this was how things would be
and therefore wasn't it a surprise? Things aren't supposed to happen according
to plan and thus when they do it's a small dislocation in the universe; clocks
are delayed a millisecond and this causes phenomena to run counter to their
         usual course,
so I should be washed free of all blame. And even if it were otherwise,
arriving someplace and forgetting one's speech isn't such a grand or unique occasion;
it's like chess. The same things happen over and over again under such different
         guises,

but you think you're keeping up with them. That serves to salve
the individual conscience and suppress the crowd's roar as effectively
as a bell-jar would. I washed the jug in some water, then
wiped it clean with a cloth. I was thinking again about all the suffering and dying
that goes on all around us, in hospitals especially. Somehow the face of the mentally
retarded woman came back to haunt me. "Oh, no, not you again!" But she was
    all the time
talking quietly to herself and couldn't have heard me anyway
with that thick partition of glass between us. But even
if she could have it wouldn't have mattered; it'd have sounded like consolation
or agreement (so there was no point in attempting these either, they'd have
been transformed into static. Best not to hear). But you can never ignore
for long the pain that comes over you from such a person, how all the wishing
in the world would only make things worse. Yes, and you are a voyeur, too,
unfortunately, and the purity of your desire could hardly be extricated
from all that. You are a voyeur with a conscience, the last thing anyone should be,
I swear. No use trying to cover your tracks using archaic words like "leman"; the
    sense
kills and you have the refrain to remind you. Sure but I was just drifting
anyway, faintly out of tune, nothing scared could have happened to me.
                                             On a

    treadmill
it would have been different, I'd have had the reward of seeing shining eyes,
knowing them directed at me. How I'd have fulfilled my promise if I'd been let go
or not, but that's a small cataclysm in a landscape now
that's no matter. I just want to be left at home—maybe something perky or melodic
will come along, who knows, and in the meantime I can irritate myself without
    causing
discomfort to others.
              As on a darkling strand when the weather improves a bit,
there was a little more to be seen than was apparent at first. The groan of pebbles

lugged back and forth by the undertow, which at first seemed temporary and quickly
turned out to be eternal wasn't made to displease me, no more than were
the hanks of pubic seaweed deposited at intervals that might well have been
predetermined, though of course they were not, no more than were the houses
irregularly staggered up the street that led away from all this, but not
too far away. I had just been having my first nightmare at the age of 59, and
           awoke refreshed
to the ordinariness of the way things didn't want to shake hands with me; it
was pleasant in my sight.
                              "Wait here a moment, I'll be right back," she called
over her shoulder. Things had been regularly falling into place
for some time, but this wasn't one of them: "Look how
little shore there's actually left." But it wasn't true, there was a broad shelf
spattered with puddles of water extending quite a ways, glittering
in the softly veiled sunlight. Does she think you too
are going to come around to her notion of things, when we touch, and glance
at each other? Or will there positively not be any sequel
to it this time? But songs, yes. They cascade
into one another. It's getting dark, I fear. We should go back
though not until you—her—have answered the riddle of the miracle, why it crests
just at this point every year, and then ceases to speak, and the silence extends it
even as far as the forever with telling tears and twilights. Tell me, did
I ever come to you, talking like this, and you received me into you, and I dwell
with you? O we were never a couple, but at last
the lantern-light pierces the horn of distress, of mayhem: you may want to
rearrange the facts now that they're getting scarce. All this points to only one
perpetrator, and that person is—and a shot rang out. The intruder sprawled
in his new pants, a helpless look on his visage, as when one from outdoors rushes in,
sees the truth, and confesses; but surely more is to come, the stain
sang in the wall, and the wall buckled. And it was all up to us co-conspirators: more
even an uncle and an aunt couldn't ask. And veiled day paled, even

as it drained into the catch basin of our collective unconscious: just who were
we to feel this way anyway, and why had anyone asked? A mystery. The clerk
sharpened his pen and put it away. But as for coming back tomorrow, that was
    wonderful,
and also in the succeeding days ahead when the losses should be more acutely visible
and the burns too. The stone house man had built upon the shore, with the
    station-master
in it.

Speaking of which the weary sap next comes to your door.
What right have you to consider yourself anything but an enormously eccentric though
not too egocentric character, whose sins of omission haven't omitted much,
whose personal-pronoun lapses may indeed have contributed to augmenting the
    hardship
silently resented among the working classes? If I thought that for a minute I'd . . . yet,
remembering how you didn't want to get up today, how warm the bed was and
    cozy, you
couldn't really begin with a proletarian, accustomed as they are to backbreaking
toil and so (you'd like to think) don't feel it that much. Besides they never read
    Henry James' novels.
Just for the sake of argument let's say I've never done an honest day's work
in my life. It's hardly heartbreaking news, not
a major concern. Calling shots
is something I've done a lot of, and I'm here to tell you as referee that too much
isn't enough, and that coldness must get boxed out by somebody
or the universe would get derailed. Besides, maybe they do feel it less, as infants
and the feeble-minded are said to. My first concern (in any case) was to build up
a graduated series of studies, leading to the alchemical perfection of one who says,
I can do that. The fabrication of it lasted nearly a lifetime,

leaving me, at the end, unable to perform the most banal act such as tying my
    shoelaces
in a double knot, and vulnerable to the japes of skeptics
who would have preferred to die a thousand deaths rather than undertake the course
of study I had so painstakingly elaborated. And as for me, sad to say,
I could never bring myself to offer my experiments the gift of objective, scientific
evaluation. Anything rather than that! So I feel I have
wandered too long in the halls of the nineteenth century: its exhibits,
talismans, prejudices, erroneous procedures and doomed expeditions are but too
    familiar
to me; I must shade my eyes from the light with my hands, the light of the explosion
of the upcoming twentieth century. Nobody asked me whether I wanted to be
    born here,
whether I liked it here, but that's hardly an excuse for cobbling a palace of
    mendacious *rêves*
into something like existence. The entry is inconspicuous, more like a sentry's box,
but the grand regularity of the insides, spoilt by a profusion of ornament, is
(however) my main contribution to the history of sitting and licking.
                                    Over the door
a weathered board scratched with impossible-to-make-out letters, and for this
he was a child and we grew up knowing him, at least some did, and he
was fair as any, and stood in open cornfields sometimes
to give the scale
to his dreaming, and the dreams of one vast civilization.
We can see the effects now in devices we use in everyday life without thinking of
    them,
in traces of the slightly altered climate and the disproportionately enormous
    effect it has had
on geography, roads and productivity. Someone in his class
should have made him a marshal. Still, he never had the courage to follow his bent
to the exclusion of petty distractions, nor they to follow him when the wind stood

in his sails, and he on the poop deck, calling, *Arise,*
ye unchained millions, and realize your consequences
only before it's too late! I'm afraid it's all busywork
for the historian of manners, now. Trash and understanding. When they collected
on the balcony, some curious, it was only to listen to the upward whoosh! of air,
     to learn
how the week of seminars had gotten canceled due to circumstances beyond our
     control,
but out of spite, actually. Whose? His or the provost's? When they said, *Does it buzz?*
he replied, yes it does. And there was an end to making arrangements. Many had
already mounted the homeward trail, headed for a warm bath and a good fuck.
     Others
noted a change in the atmosphere: surely it was lighter, but thinner?
So you tell yourself you're going to show yourself and say no to yourself
before witnesses are dragged in to recant. It works so well—how *do* you manage it,
dear? Being able to go in and out at any point, I mean. In this case
it's back to the hurricane. When we last looked in though
there were party streamers suspended from ceiling fixtures, and everything
seemed to be in full swing. Now, Marsha's baby occupies center stage.
Whodunit? Dunno. But let's listen in: "For the fourth time I want you
to go over there where the washing is and stand the nasty question on its head.
I mean, what are mussels?" And so it goes, down to the loading and unloading,
the pretty bleak exteriors. For some, it causes eye cramps. But the boldest line
on today is Cedric's "Hey how'd we get this way, eyeful? And the fault of whose buns
ran it aground in Norwalk, if only you'd had an antenna out for the main, the central
occasion and dash after it like a slaphappy Weimaraner and diddle it, 'cos
it's ours, dig? Of course, after I was 'slimed' for the first time, and by
you, no less, I became increasingly withdrawn for years and the case dragged
through the courts before finally being settled. And by what right
do I imagine you this spring day?"

                    Mostly the others are more secretive, or were,

until this new bombshell hit the stands. Now, full of remorse, we ask ourselves
what we could have done to prevent the calamity. But there was nothing,
of course, beyond waiting it out, under a dripping awning, on the beach.
The "elegancy" which Malone imposed upon it was in the direction of that
        generalization
dear to the eighteenth-century heart, which the modern temperament finds
so uncongenial. Clearly we were to blame in some way we cannot know
other than by divination or recourse to charlatans, which, I'd better say
right off, is totally out of the question. But when fear pelts down
one forgets such resolves. I was ever
determined not to reveal myself a stoolie. I had sat in a metal chair before,
yet had always assumed that with age a mingled straggling peace and dignity
came along. Even in my late forties I patiently awaited
this. After dinner she played Kjerulf. We sipped tea, looking at each other.
I find appealing the quality of danger
inherent in thunder, though of course it's actually in the lightning,
which I don't much like at all. I'll take my jacket off now, and be off.
Another day we read the thunder its own prepared statement.
The effect was stupefying. I always do get that feeling
of being prepared for anything but this, usually followed by a postscript
about deciding to mend my ways, abjure evil delight, from this day forward.
This, however, was something else. I may never speak the truth again,
knowing it to be compounded of false mottoes and *aperçus*, and that trying
should be good enough. You get A for effort, but the road to hell is paved
with good intentions. But I'll take the blight,
thanks. I'm good at working under pressure,
as indeed we all must be.

§

153

Sure, he was still at it by the time the others left. Some protection.
We had just time to get out. I had mislaid the thermometer. And pill. I bet
your sweet life I had to do it, to come up with something, for weren't we all equals
under the law? And how much should I let that excuse him? Ethical questions
were never my strong suit, but I wished to pass the gravy anyway, and in that
I was successful. Never to come round here again. Listen to politics
or someone filing on the word, and then a gush as from a well
occurs and no one is fit to stretch anymore. The old bomb was
having its say, I didn't know they allowed that, I thought it was still
that they outmoded it, sometime in the fifties. But to me, the last war
is World War II. I thought youth began then, is still going on, but for printing that
I'd be "libel" to legal action, so I pretend it's not like my youth anymore,
that things have grown up and gray. One or two friends and I, well we
get together and talk about it no oftener than once a month. You see,
the colors are in here in the dark too, only you can't see them, just feel them.
Don't touch. But these are in some way more satisfying than the others,
though also more eclectic. Did I say hectic? Yes, they are that too . . .

The wheat was the color of old men, the robin . . . Well these are what I had got
to offer you; I suppose it doesn't make any difference now because you have
     something new
that was not in the catalog I have. Something sweet, turning over, something
     unbuttoned.
But now there is no dose you can tolerate, no
sitting in the sun like a chunk of wood or a large broken fungus; it scarcely
matters which. See, I'm like you, a believer. At the same time I want to believe in
     things
that are endless, even though we don't get to see them every day, that are
what color is to a colorless surface, which I believe I have inhabited

once, or once upon a time. My politics shouldn't matter. It's my finger
that should—it's here I'll take my stand. I want over and over
to tell you what we are is *digital*, that no other form exists, at least if it does it
is as a function to the other great, existing forms, and they are already published,
it seems, in places. I have no desire other than to survive the endless extremes
of heat and cold. For a dollar I could put it in the mail to you,
my little tract, but so many others wanted it and spurned it. But I'm
thinking of you anyway, shall not go away, lest another be duller
than I'm, and I'm not trusting myself to get away
except on a lawn roller moving one to two miles per hour, and that
means we shall have to change when we get there, if we're tired, or be hired
by some straw boss and be sent to the rockpile for our pains, our talents
in getting lively others to talk about ourselves, how
they came down from Canaan in a wood car, and all was a frozen dump.
Why don't any of you want to come back with me,
where I see, from nesting, where the tree is? Long I've labored . . .
But others come along and do the job so much quicker, I'm almost
out of breath, and arranged to go home with them for the night.
I'd like more children around,
but that's it, not everything can be right, there must be a small hole
near the base, and all must get along, and not try to cover it
with anything. A shawl or turban would of course help.
But what does it matter if no one sees,
if there is no one to take attendance, and meanwhile the dam is overflowed
by some water, even as it comes rolling even to your feet. And what do you say
about it then, what ask for? If there are ideals in this society, let them speak
or afterward hold their peace since no job is going to get done until whoever
is here has explained the technical language in ways that I
and a chambermaid can understand. We've had so little help,
of late, been so understaffed, that even quite important logs
have rolled into the fireplace unbidden, and I

was never going to screw again, though there may have been error there, until
    the time
inscribed in colored crayons, upon the wall. And a distant
sister comes to take over, nurse you back to health and heresy
of your time, put one interest ahead of all others: staying still! Not talking!
    Pretty soon
it's everyone's job, the obligation to have a work-force be here
at times when no one else's is. Peace, and a thread of breath: that's all
they want; there's no reason to be excited
by their shout. And the poor little ones get some attention; it's as well,
you might think, and are sent off to the hills
once they have recuperated a bit from the noise and accident; oh what
disaster is closer to us today, and how do some others cope
in the meantime, until the vice-president can be here? And what cops
are talking together outside? Under the grape-arbor? Ah well it's no more of a
    season
now than it ever was; this year has got to be flooded out, and then it's
up to who can play. The morris-dances
are superseded, and others, who wish to join in, cannot. That is all what our rime
    is about,
we who are running, falling, reacting. In case the coat of burrs got overstated
we can sing operetta, or resurrect pliant golfers,
trying one's hand too at vanity in order to catch everything else.

Meanwhile the meat has been prepared and divided.
It was time to climb up, to pull the ladder up, having construed pith in the
    latest verbal
assaults from onlookers who wished to be crowned too. And that was really all
    it was about:

why, then, did it get blown out of context? In another decade there'd be no duel,
no stony silence in the media, only a little sunlight and frowning
before standing up again, past true forgetting. But in the meantime
its warped head wanders; there can never be a peaceful settlement, only further
reprisals and squeamishness, each day a curdled dawn, and no one remembers
why we were angry, only that a strict vengeance must be enacted. Even those
on the deck of a steamer departing for new free ports whose stone breakwaters
        will not have learned
of the mystery before are like sleepwalkers amid the gaiety, the greetings: did we say
it was to end here? And the sky of late spring and promising summer, deeply
saturated as always during times of war and occupation, promises no quick
        unraveling
of the skein of secret misery lobbed from generation to generation, though it
        does promise
much in the way of atmospheres and easy repose, and so may lighten the
burden for future cliff-dwellers, when it shall be seen and printed that all our care
is quaint anachronisms or prompt-scripts for retro chic. Yet they too, followers,
become lost in ever-narrowing canyons as day wanes, unwilling
to relinquish the post of court-historian to a younger and grubbier clientele,
and so history constantly dwindles, although one can still feel remarkably fit and
        well-adjusted
to life in an era more decadent than anything that has preceded it. These stylized
floral motifs the world offers aren't meant to be consumed, mindlessly,
before the waltz ends and fashion begins again; neither
is it a comment on one to have lost them, to arrive without memory at twilight,
which in any case spares no one. Blips from the maritime
provinces made it all disturbingly real: that anyone should have to die
so that we may stay on here, sodden but alive, fortunate
to be able to contemplate our mortality from a distance amid kindness
and late imperial emblems, golden dregs of another civilization
than the one we gulped down just a short time ago.

Its vanity pardons no one though, and there are other cudgels for defending
one's secret inclination than wisps of hope, transplanted, never acclimated,
that betray you at the end. How fast the children have grown this year!
No lovers undefeated? No time to return to the technical college? Then
you should have made a promise not to seek redress. The charm can't contain
      you now.
Apologies to all and sundry, and for the green that impedes
whatever I do in my writing, like a bias. *Why* hold that tiger? Or perform six other
acts before lunch, when all writing is putting aside something
in one's lap, like a sandwich, juggling priorities? But at least in this case it went well
until the long, late-afternoon-solemn street led first
to a shiver beyond it and next to a ship absurdly bedded in the snow, like a guidepost.
And then, finally, the year's shifting gears got to me, though I know
enough to be prepared for whatever explodes in your face. Still,
nobody amuses me anymore. I think now that in another time less would have
      been made
of all this. Formerly I was of a different opinion. But we moderns have to "leave
      our mark"
on whatever we say and do; we can let nothing pass without a comment
of some kind. Even rural lapses like water provoke us
to exquisite nitpicking, and then we don't know where we are when we stop
for the night. It could be one of the United States, it could be a European country.
But we are so riled at what has come secretly to possess us that it can't make any
      difference
to the maggot in one's sight, the flea in one's ear: all is basically kindling for the late
greater conflagration in which we think we shall see our destiny: our fate and death
as one. And when a shining thing approaches, rush out to meet it half-cocked
and laughing hysterically with worry. "This is my psychopomp; I ordered it!"
      But all that
is writing at the margin where daddy-long-legs tend to congregate. When we need
wackier prescriptions, we'll let you know. Meanwhile, be one of those

on whom nothing is lost. Organize your thoughts in random lines and, later on
down the road, paginate them. You'll see bluebells and cowslips on every hill; even
dragonflies will have become a thing of wonder, as long
as you don't get too close, and let water run through it all. What the hell! We're
in here having a fine time, our satisfaction pierces heaven's summit, and there
     are only
a few more who need to be drugged or convinced. As long as we're on this planet
the thrill never ceases. Even a garage can be a propitious place; a mechanic's
whistle from under a car can add to the spectrum of consternation suspended, and
making faces in the weeds. As long as we are never who we are ever going to be
the bind obtains and life on the edge of a knife has its own kind of
     remuneration,
so tenuous is the balance that keeps one foot caught in a misunderstanding
of someone's making. On the other
hand to walk away from it is the grave good face to austerity and fundamental
decisions that were reached long ago in the childhood of ambassadors in the
     nursery
of stars, and we can't avoid our reflection in these. It's come to get us, to take us
to the ceremony.

To the "newness" then, all subscribe, albeit with a few reservations. We have
     been living
in Herkimer for some time. The quiet plenitude exuded by fat, lettuce-colored stalks
is one thing, a haven, yet always in the imagination a hasp is loose,
something catches. One might, it is true, have preferred isles edged for miles and
     miles
with seabirds' feathers, and a smart-looking interior. But to give up what
has been offered is not a man's way. Similarly, when a drunken interlocutor
gets you and your best friend mixed up, the question is not whether to proceed into

the misunderstanding, but how to extend the frame
more or less grouping us as we sat before.
                                    There was no luster then. But the
        suggestiveness
of both, blowhard and gawker, made it seem that a real element of choice
were sequestered, down there, near the root, as the shadow of an elegy fanned out
over the slag, enormous to this day. And just as one can remember a foreign
word but not the synonym for it in one's own language, it became a misleading
index of one's intelligence, just a little too imposing to be taken home
and placed on exhibit there. I talked to the governor's men
but though I could make myself understood in any language, it was without the
        foundation
that hope supplies when something is going well. Further negotiations were useless.
Besides, it seemed that the cinnabar headlands were not now a convergence;
that trophies other than this one would be talked about when the time came for that,
that no more daunting voyage could have shaken the recruit's resolve;
        meanwhile the press-gang
cheered on the puny efforts at repeal that I and my wimpish cohorts advocated, then
resolved to push through the ratification process. And, unfortunately, we all
        looked alike; hence,
no one took us seriously or thrust chicken sandwiches on us. It was all a sad day,
though a merry one insofar as we were going home, albeit unwillingly.
        "Unwillingly,
O queen, I left your shore." Yet she saw that none of us left empty-handed; I
        still have
that souvenir, and therefore cannot decry the fate that brought me to this pass, alone,
untended, with still some forty miles to go before I can call my journey ended.
There were some who mocked us, and some that threw pebbles at our backs. But
        these
we scarcely noticed, buckled into our seats, laughing at the dream that took us
        back to the

foundations of real fear where the story must be lived if it is to matter at all to others.
That of course was no concern of ours; we thought *we* were the others, observing
our exemplary adventures through a wall
of water that splits from time to time, revealing the real nature of the operation,
    that it is not
a place of entertainment, rather a swamp, from which one emerges,
before lying on the grass for a long time, getting one's bearings and indeed doing
    anything
to buy time and fool our jailers until the moment that becomes a nocturne and
    precipitates
the glabrous drop that will satiate us and send us home, muttering
of the winds and suchlike. Inside this privileged attitude a revolutionary spark
    asserted
its rights; a trail of powder blazed there where but a moment before cool arches
led from one to the other and the view of hillsides wavered as in a bath
of sodium silicate, and seemed permanent. But that was the governor's trick to
    trip you up,
make you confess what he already knew, before returning
overwhelmed to your alcove. All these officials had a stake in the matter, and it was
moreover their tactic to give you rope enough to hang yourself; if you wanted
    to braid a ladder
with it, why that was all right too, provided somebody saw it and wrote about it.
    So for
sixteen years I dazzled the constituents with sayings of a country I had never
    seen; they knew I
raved but thought it must always be so when men dreamed, but my darker
purpose never surfaced. And on the day when I was set free on the sand
and told to run no one could remember my name; as soon as I realized I was beyond
the range of their small arms I could relax and saunter, or, as the mood progressed,
bury my face in my hands trying to remember what it was, what gable had
    afflicted me now, or

how I should be caring about the move across the ever-shrinking circles, as though
I was going to enter 'em, and not let the enemy hear of any further predicament
regarding me or those I formerly associated with as long as everyone kept silent as
their part of the bargain, and I too dreamed, loosely, because I didn't want the
landscape and hares to remember they'd once seen me if asked. And the
    landmark decision I
helped instigate came tolling through the last several years of thatch and plaster
    and was as
my trademark; everybody knew me and I had only to walk through a hole
for it to become named as a piece of the life I was hoping to publish. No there
    were some
who were unhappy with this, and not content with tormenting me, actually
    made me see
there was no difference, no other way I could have gone on being
what once I had been. But the echoes of my calm egocentricity rolled over
    them too;
it was as if I had never held on to the blank stubs of my raffle tickets; in my
    composure
anything odd I said turned over and was revealed as the reverse of a truth that
    was something else,
and in such wise I was able to live for close to a year, in my
caboose, and no one suspected my ruse or fatal intelligence; they had other things
    to do,
and besides it was obvious I wasn't such a bad sort, we should all have to cotton
    to each other
and in so doing satisfy the chain destiny had prepared for us, the note
about to fall due. And I laughed
at the leaves floating in the cistern, that they too were my reward, and someday
all of us would come together in joyful earnest, for what it could do, and then
    my plans
would be better laid, and the daughters of those that were around us

would thrive specially too, and in becoming lead me into the cloud of chaff that was
to be my recompense, besides anything I really cared to do,
which could always be arranged, and anyway the future would be better for it
if I could just take my feet off the pedals and keep them there awhile.
And behold it all became good, and everybody recognized it. And the historians
    have had their say,
only now is too much done about it, and there is defeat, and fears about not
remembering. And so it will not pass away.

V

Nothing is required of you, yet all must render an accounting.
I said I was out hunting in the forest. How can it be that a man
can sup his fill, and still all around him find emptiness and drowsiness,
if he must go to the grave this way, unattended? Yet certainly
there are some bright spots, and when you listen to the laughter
in the middle of these it makes for more than a cosmetic truth, an invitation
to chivalry ringed by the dump fires of our deliberate civilization that has
got some things going for it—that invented neighborliness, for instance?
Then the paltry painted guest goes away, leaving behind the screed
she omitted to read. What's in it for us? Out of this school was sucked a
    philosophy
that didn't impel to action. A back-burner sort of thing. But if people had but
kept track of it that would have been something, someone could have framed
a memorandum. But they quickly find out what the traffic will bear
and are soon asleep in the midst of it, and the next call to action is considered passé
and no one will believe you represent the right cause. A piece of webbing
is nailed to the ground; ring-grass
invades its orient extremity; even these criteria have to be put away
until later. The hangar gets unbearably hot and very smelly.
Meanwhile the new green cascades silently and as it were invisibly.
Something has been said. You're right about that. But no two people
can agree on what it means, as though we were sounding boards

for each childish attempt at wireless communication the gods can invent,
and so return to our refectory. But I didn't know but what if I
didn't hang around a little longer the thrust
would be vouchsafed to *me* this time and of course as its public
repository I would use it to further the interests of all men and women,
not just some. And it left the same message. It was as though
it never got my previous message. Sure, I'm still not yet compromised
but there was so much in those fierce screens that ought to have lived
as an example to conceal more and then to have it break out of control and be put
down again if ever I could will myself to wish it, instead of lingering
like a daisy on muck. Take out my tricycle for a spin and return it
before anyone missed me. Yet, as I said, I didn't know. The old men at the urinal
spat, not wanting word to get out. All my links with a certain past were severed.
I let fall the book I had been reading, *The Radiator Girls at Strapontin Lodge,*
as so much gift to the giver of idiosyncrasies which when adopted
sift down like bran on rutted earth to accumulate
in whorls, and I thought how I could give no account
of these latest days. It was as though I had gone through a bout of amnesia.
Now I was ready to put the gloves on again, but wasn't it too late?
Wasn't the amnesty or amnesia of my own decreeing and applicable not even
to one, to me, and in that case weren't we all excused
from class? And yet the board of governors certified me; I became a vicious citizen,
not even to blame for what ills dunces harbored
in God knows what unimaginable slums, for as long as I chose to occupy my seat
cooperating with the forces of eternal law and order yet unwilling
to compromise friends, neighbors, orderlies, the giraffe at the zoo,
who even now moves toward me on unbending legs,
though his designs are far from clear. From whatever is happy and not
unholy, lead: the plan of the porch is quite an obvious one, and you know
what sliding doors mean and wherefore gutters conduct rain
to the abject earth, and turn around and absorb the shock of hearing the truth

told, once more, on an unforgettable day in early June,
which shall be all we need ever know of hearing quarrels inside out and then
reversing them so the abstract argument is pure and just again, a joy to many.

How much luckier I am, though, than they, who can see where I'm stumbling to
     during the day
and can rein in at night, between hedges. It's like
dangling far above the city streets, a kind of peace if you don't spoil it
by losing patience. Sure enough, other fun began while I was gone, a kind of
     imaginative
recycling of the days I'd crumpled and tossed out, and then their
dated shenanigans came to
seem crisp and well-presented, focussed, cropped; none of the "careful
     draftsman" in me could
cavil at that. Besides it was nice just being outdoors with something to say. An excuse
like a birthmark arose and flowered, still swimming upward past
the layers of the different civilizations, to Sun Lake. I could trundle my shopping
     cart past
the wicket and still be there, off the hook. I don't mind being mesmerized even for
fairly long periods but this was like playing tic-tac-toe with an automated
stone saint; the mock-orange note in it was strong and I'd come, I
remembered, chiefly to see my own reflection. Now, where was I? Where'd I put that
ticket of readmission to the bathers, who by this time were streaming out
in twos and threes. "Show us how to open a book like that." We gave them coffee
when it didn't go fast enough. Things seemed to pick up after that, though I felt
   a twinge:

   §

was it going to do it for me, this time, and them? Might we be forced to split up,
and if so, which half of the ladder is left standing? You don't want to hear it.
        And still
the cloister extends, deeper and deeper into the dream of everyday life that was our
beginning, and where we still live, out in the open, under clouds stacked up in a
        holding pattern
like pictures in a nineteenth-century museum: forgive us
our stitch of frivolity in the fabric of eternity if only so that others
can see how shabby the truth isn't and make their depositions accordingly, regulating
the paths over which we have no control now, speaking out of concentrated
politeness into an ear which wishes to hear, but once we have finished
what we had to say (and we have nothing to say) the moment and any
        afterthoughts are scooped up
as though by a steam shovel and deposited *over there*, not out of sight.
And the contentious are sometimes with us as a smooth pavane on glassy but
        profoundly
turbulent waters. How to keep it going
when all is trembling violently anyway, the air and all things in it? Shouldn't we
abandon them? But no these are
pointlessly fussy caveats sunk, so as to test one, in the great gray
fabric of the unwinding highway: don't let its apparent dignity fool you, and besides
they're free, and can and do say whatever they want to you; that doesn't
mean you have to respond in kind, but it helps. Someone is working on it,
providing heat in summer and air conditioning in winter, and get-well
notes arrive in every post; the top
of the volcano has been successfully glued back on, and who is to say we aren't
invited? The invitation, after all, arrived too, that was your name
beautifully chiselled into it. And ideas like fire
struck too quickly from flint seem to matter: your house or my house,
this time?
        I really think it's my turn,

but the variations don't let you proceed along one footpath normally; there are
too many ways to go. I guess that's what I meant. Why I was worried,
all along, I mean, though I knew it was superfluous and that you'd love me for it
or for anything else as long as I could sort out the strands that brought us together
and dye them for identification purposes further on, but you
didn't have to remain that generalized. A few anomalies
are a help sometimes, confetti that gets lost in the cracks
of some conversation and then you have to take it back again to the beginning
and start all over again, but that's normal, it's no cause for alarm, there are
more people out there than before. If you can think constructively, cogently,
on a spring morning like this and really want to know the result in advance, and can
accept the inroads colorful difficulties can sometimes make as well as all the
fortunate happening, the unexpected pleasures and all that, then there's no
   reason not to
rejoice in the exterior outcome, sudden
mountain-face, the abrupt slide
into somewhere or other. It will all twist us
closer together, under heaven, and I guess that's what you came about. See these
polished stones? I want them and I want you to have them. It's time, now.

So that's it, really. How all that fluff got wedged in with the diamonds in the
   star chamber
makes for compelling reading, as does the heading "Eyesores," though what
   comes under it,
e.g., "Nancy's pendant," is a decidedly mixed bag. The proper walk must be aborted
and tangled hope restored to its rightful place in the hierarchy of dutiful devotions
for it to matter at all to "the likes of" us, and get booted to the rear
of the compartment. We were talking about cats. I said you should have one

not so much for companionship as for the extreme urgency of not letting it out
        of the bag,
if you should be so lucky as to possess one of those too. You always thank me
for my suggestions even when I can see they haven't gone over too well, and this
was one of those times. We chatted some more about cats and other pets
and then parted on an amiable note, what I would call one. And all during the
        succeeding
weeks there was no word, nothing on the radio, what we call the wireless. You'd
        think a line
like "HUNT MISSING GIRL" might have turned up in the papers, but the
        actual situation
was otherwise. A standoff. A phantom so strange in its implications it defies
. . . classification. Otherwise, how his beans were cooked
made absolutely no difference to him. In fact he seemed to lose interest in his
        surroundings
daily. I remember including that in one of my reports. If he asked for a nail file
it would be to stab playfully at the pillow, or occasionally to clean his nails,
never to file them. Once I even saw him reading a detective novel upside down.
I was too upset to include *that* in my report, as you may imagine. And secretly he
wheedles favors out of us; the older nurses are more susceptible. If he wants to
wind up sidelined, in the dugout, that is OK with me, but I don't see why *I*
        should be expected
to sign the warrant for his release. I have other, more important, things to do, besides.
Getting that bit of lacquer repaired is just one of them, but you get my drift,
I fear, then too I've traditionally been the indulgent, mild-mannered one,
who thought nothing of taking an afternoon off to play golf if the weather was right
as it is so seldom in this inclement land. When I asked about the new monitors
someone brought in I wasn't expecting a sermon on the necessity of staking out one's
territory the very same day, but there it came, with a hurricane in its pocket for
        good measure.

And when no one was betting on horses, there were the nags to feed,
the grooms' quarters to be kept in proper order, liveries to be pressed—it all came
gushing down on me like a bushel of affectionate children. It is lucky I am
old enough to keep my head, faced with the demands on my time. Even a computer
would get riled sometimes. Now I am more interested in "easy living,"
though more than ever feeling a need to keep up appearances, impress the neighbors
with the latest electronic *trouvaille*. Yet I never let down my defenses
for a moment. I am what some people would call "hard," though
I'm really a pussycat underneath the austere façade. Speaking of cats, when was the last
time you spoke to one, calling it by its name? Out here on the prairie things are
        much too quiet
though we all know each other and share memories and stratagems
for coping with loneliness and disloyalty from time to time. In some ways
it's a life, or something you'd have no difficulty recognizing as such, but I wonder,
how are they going to fit me in at the end? Will my birdcage be draped
with some expensive Liberty fabric to suggest eternal peace, just as I was getting used
to the lively round of tea-parties and exhibits
some are over-attached to, but when you think
about it, what's wrong with a little pudding? Sprinkled with coconut, perhaps?
And then in the evening you get down to business, but you can't think clearer then.
Here there is no mist to admonish one, no pretzel sticks either,
and one knows very well what one wants to be
and can imagine a fancier existence anywhere. This has to get broken off here
for the reason things do get broken off: it's amusing. Love,
The Human Pool Table.

Sometimes to stimulate interest in other titles we
try to encourage a different angle such as the Near East with its walled, secret
        gardens,

jacaranda petals that fall all day into the basin. And the hours,
peeled off one after the other like onion skin, yet there is always more:
some curve up ahead. In fact
we never see all there is to see
which is good for business too: keeps the public returning
these days of swiftly eroding brand loyalty, so you can say: I beat him up,
my competitor, and now I'm ready to do business with him again: such
is the interesting climate we live in, all
shocks one minute, all smiles and surprises the next. I think I'll have the chicken
    salad oriental. I'll
wager you haven't one client in seven who can identify this, though the whole
    world knows of it,
this quite tiny key to success I hold in my hand. When the codger
returns I'll brusquely bring the question up again and you'll see. It's cooler
over here; the light forms a film at the windows
I first took for a curtain, a rash that won't wear off. Wait, now
he's ready to talk business. I have, sir, a handle on the truth
that could be of keen interest to you, a matter of considerable importance.
You can feel it when the lake is up and swans go flapping off
on various absurd errands, or when the phone rings and you hear his voice
before picking up the receiver, saying, It's me, I'm glad I waited
till you were in a different frame of mind, for truly this makes all the difference;
    no one
calls the woman who walks silently away, but later in the night
there are twists of tears and it seems as if someone shares your nervousness
about the awkward pauses that might ensue and has arrived at a plan of drastic
    action:
whisking the tablecloth off the laden table without disturbing a spoon is only
    part of it.
Giving up habits like compulsive hand-washing is another. Because you have no
    idea how

imperious their demands are; nothing can get closer to you as long as they are in
     the car-port
even though they too have nothing to say
and cannot justify their existence.

Other pleasures are folding the pillow and gazing mournfully into the face of
     the electric clock
when everything springs apart quite naturally and scrawled forms of people
are seen pacing the square in different directions; sometimes
one will hold on to another's head and then let go: it's my Sonata
of Experience, and I wrote it for you. Here's how it goes: the first theme is
     announced,
then fooled around with for a while and goes and sits over there. Soon the second
arrives, less appealing than the first or so it seems but after you get to know it you find
it deeper and somehow more human, like the plain face of an old lady who has
     seen much
but who has never been known to utter an opinion on anything that happens to
     her: quite
extraordinary, in fact. Then comes a hiatus in the manuscript:
the last bits of it keep seeming to move farther and farther away, like houses
on a beach one is leaving in a speeding motorboat: wait, though!
isn't that them we're approaching now? Of course—we had been going around
     in a circle
all the time, and now we have arrived at the place of resolution. The stakes are high
now, but you couldn't tell it from the glum air of things: bored crows, seedlings.
And then, what passion
brought you to your knees? Suddenly your whole face is bathed in tears, though
     no one

saw you cry. This kind of makes me review my whole plan of action up to now;
     fishing around
for a handkerchief to hand someone does that to a person, I think, don't you?
And it will mean staying up later which in turn will screw up
tomorrow's well-laid plans, and then suddenly everything ends in a climax, or a
     cataract.
I think this *is* the way it was supposed to be, though I can't be sure now, so much
     has happened;
it will look better on a cassette, which is where I wanted it anyway, so I guess
we can go home now, each to his own bed, for each of us has one: that's what
     "calling it a night" means.
But I never meant to disturb anything, or harm a hair on your head: that would
     have been false
to our beginnings, and nothing could stand up to that, nothing good I mean.

As it builds, the power changes too, but in the
same direction it was carelessly aimed in long ago, before any of us got involved
with what we now consider our living, when it was free. And the strain grows,
     steadily,
though there are many scenes played for comic relief and the classic agendas are still
re-enacted when people get together. Not quite late-twentieth-century panic, but
     sobering in its
simple difference which can scarcely be demonstrated. All the people we knew
     and the songs
we sang are on our side, sinking imperceptibly
along with us into Old Home Week. Except it's not. And we cannot see the bottom
of these issues; they have outgrown us; which made the eye in the church shine
     even brighter

when it finally opened. Meanwhile, over the scruffy skies of New York, a doubt hangs
like a jewel, a melancholy melon-color that could be the correct shade of
    mourning
in heaven, pitting all that we said against us. Why, it's right there in the *procès verbal*,
only I don't feel too good. I just want to be absorbed in countries you were never
allowed to develop a taste for, yet I have no reason to go anywhere,
to be at your side, every place seems as mortally insipid
as every other place, and I've got used to living, like a toothache; I can stand
what's coming, but that doesn't mean I don't have to like it. Some mornings are
    quite pleasant:
a Florentine wonderment drips from the sky as putti with picnic baskets descend
to the enameled sward, and I don't have to ask you how near you think that
    lighthouse is,
or the blond warehouse: you find me in them. Is it asking too much
to want to be loved, just a little, and then to be satisfied with that? Of course not,
but the police are everywhere. You can't even order a drink without feeling one
    of them breathing
down your neck. And you apologize profusely, like the ridiculous twit you are.
Where is it written that men must go out in the afternoon without a hat?

In the real world things were going along about as well as could be expected, that is,
not quite satisfactorily. We were deceived in our reckoning,
but could still salvage some things like a decent emolument and self-respect. But
    in many ways
things were different now. Even the coastline had changed,
and the protective vacuum-packing around long-established major
    confrontations was no longer
mandatory. One sat at a kind of grillwork that used to be the kitchen table,

while outside hives exploded and buzzing insects darkened the air and we
 thought we knew
the year we graduated from high school, yet everything was suspended in an
 agitated trance.
Only, I knew where I wanted to go: to some mountains in the south covered
 with pine forests
and creeper. There, the silence causes you to will what you wanted to know without
exactly knowing if it was OK.
                              Here, curvaceous rocks brandish us; the squeals
 of "Put me *down!*"
are mere grace-notes in this battle of stupid titans. Strangely, a few amenities do
 survive,
enough to seem to give the lie to so much stinking chaos which, since it hasn't
 overturned
everything, is therefore perhaps not what its pennant in the sky proclaims it to be:
walks by creeks, for instance. Yet by enabling all creatures to become something
 different,
not necessarily their opposite, the proposed bifurcating leads in time to impossible
extremities one could never apostrophize anticipating a benign outcome due
 to the dreamlike
imaginings at the center that produced them. Waves, like weather currents on
 the map,
drift and coagulate above us, like "the swan-winged horses of the skies,
with summer's music in their manes," absolving the map of all responsibility to
 present itself,
to be read as a guide, and offering in its stead only the inane fumes of incense
spiritual masturbation set alight, long ago, and this is the bread, the palaces of
 the present,
a time that cannot tend itself. Each year the summer dwindles noticeably, but
 the Reagan

administration insists we cannot go to heaven without drinking caustic soda on
    the floor
of Death Valley as long as others pay their rent and have somewhere to go
    without thinking,
behind the curtain of closing down all operations. It's all right, I
like doing the housework naked and can see nothing wrong with it,
nor do I feel ashamed of it. I'll be all right when the government goes away; its
police state may not recognize me, or, if it does, may just shrug. What can I want,
anyway? Besides cashing in my federal insurance policy, that is. But as usual life
    is a dream
of blackbirds slowly flying, of people who come to your door needing help or merely
wanting to attack you so they can go away and say contact was made and it's
your day in the barrel.
                            Those of us who did manage to keep control over our
    personal affairs
before it was all over are obviously not going to testify anyway. What would we
    have said?
That we confronted the monster eyeball to eyeball and blinked first but only
after a decent interval had elapsed and were then excused from completing the
    examination
before defenestration became an issue? I thought I knew all about you and everything
everybody could do to me but this hiatus is sui generis and I know not how to read it
like braille and must forever remain behind in my solicitations, derelict in my duties,
until a child explains it all to me. And then I'll weep
at mountainscapes, if it isn't too late. But say,
where are you going, and why do you walk that way? Oh, I'll be all right, provided
you shut up and don't read too much into the dog's picture. After all,
the mutt said he wanted it taken, and in the backyard, so how was I to know
there'd be hell to pay for even this seeming indulgence? And how did I get away
after fourteen years? I'm afraid that's one you'll have to save for the answer man,
    besides,

my time is up and nothing too terrible has happened, only clouds, wind, stone,
    sometimes
a distant engine, purring in the morning fog, before the others are up, but I can see it.
It unwinds shelteringly.
                    But there were dreams to sell, ill didst thou buy:
not the man walking, the woman sitting on the toilet, the tuba-player unscrewing
    the mouthpiece
of his instrument and blowing into it, not the azaleas blooming in tubs; but the
    three policemen and the man
scratching his groin, turning to say something to someone you couldn't see; the
    women
who wandered up to you at a cookout, waiting for you to give them an
    affectionate
peck on the cheek; the marching band in Rio, and the one in New Orleans, who
    knew
the music very well, and played it as they walked; the African violets you called
    violettes
du Cap, white, pink and blue, doing nicely in a northern window: these, for
    your trouble,
you may have mastered and accomplished much else besides, not least turning
    yourself from a
slightly unruly child into a sophisticated and cultivated adult with a number of books
to his credit and many more projects in the works; as well as the unattractive
    dreamer,
stained with sleep, who grasps at these as they elude him, and grasps at still others
which elude him not, all the time swilling the taste of one in his mouth. Forgetful,
you hang up the receiver allowing others to get through: in your garden
there may have been much confusion but also attentive things growing, now cut
    adrift,
floundering for lack of direction from you. And we see it even in the tall houses
that fan out from here: each has its family

who are not much concerned with you, but to whom a truce was offered, and
who missed out on it

because of misplaced consideration for you; and then in the dark forests that
slant down

ravines quite close to the town, whose emptiness you could have peopled
merely by taking them up, in conversation; and the vast, greenish-gray seas
punctuated

with scudding whitecaps that are a mystery and will always remain so, but you
could have

addressed yourself to that, at least, included them in some memorial address
at the proper time, and so saved a speck of righteousness for your otherwise
unproductive antics, summoned

dazed spirits "out of hell's murky haze, heaven's blue hall," accommodated them even
as you sat beside me, reading or listening to music. Thus, it becomes time to relax
e'en so. Funny, isn't it? The last thing on your list, and now
it is being approached even as afternoon makes room for evening, when all our
aspirations shall be quietened. And if no post arrives, no hens cluck,
then it shall be just as if it had happened. Why? Because it's completed. Don't you
see the light, seeing the light? Now you see it, now you don't,
is about right, having given up all lust, all hope.

                                         There is a time for trying on
new clothes.

Yet the spirits are still angry that you woke them, if that's what you did.
Dreaming a dream to prize—way to go, Thomas L. It matters not how puke-
encrusted

the areaway, how charged with punishments the jazz-inflected scroll—this *is*
your time, by golly,

so change your clothes and get it right. THIS IS AN ILLUSTRATION OF
SOMETHING.

What people never really wanted to talk about—Stonehenge. Last year it was a
phantom's

breath upset you. Incorporate it—no second chance will be given
but what an old man said, quietly sitting at a coffee table, eyes shielded from the light.
A blast of gramophone music veers into the shutters from time to time. In those
    days and
in that time you had to have a sister and brother and be known. Now anyone
may play, but the stakes, alas, are much higher. Few
can afford to lose. Yet you see brothers, and sons, caught in the lure of it,
swapping new clothes for food, in short doing all the things you were warned against,
like talking to strangers. I like that. I only wish more of 'em would listen to me,
    but they
too have their business to attend to, curious as it seems, even as your mouth waters
at the sight of one of them, who hurries on, unfeeling. It's at night they come back,
once they know they've got you, or can have you, and then the caterwauling begins
unchecked. How would you like a plastron front to wear with this? Of course
    you wouldn't,
but that don't keep none of them from trying to play the Ripper, more shitted against
than shitting, so then they *do* rise up, and it can be one hell of a sight,
especially for those unaccustomed to it. I prefer to sit here and "rest" my eyes.
Usually my hunches are good, but last week comes one of 'em, and they always
asks you for something, begs a little jam or some string, and once you give it
you're in their power. But you knew *that*. Then the fun begins in earnest, blows rain
down from all over, chopping-block sounds, you think mechanically of Mary
    Stuart and Lady
Jane Grey, holding on to your forelock, cap in hand, of course. I don't know how long
the mist and smog have overlain this city, the dreaded heat, rising out of the sewers,
that can seem like the odor of fresh-baked buttered rolls. Then you must go to it again
and fill out a new application, for they have mislaid the first.
                                 We nightingales

sing boldly from our hearts, so listen to us:

    §

First, a saxophone quartet told me we have lived too much
in the minds of others, have too much unguaranteed capital on deposit there.

Why are you here? Why did you scream?

 Only that one told me a new-laid owl's egg is sovereign
against the gripes, and now I find you here too. I have found you out. You seem
convinced the killer is one of us. Why? Did a drowned virgin
tell you that, or Tim the ostler, or the one-eyed hay-baler
with a hook for a hand? Or was it something else—some letter
you might have received from some distant land
where all is peace under the umbrella-pines and a serpent guards
the golden apples still? Seal it didst thou,
to send it back across the water as a sigh
to those unknowable?
I'll be perfectly frank with you. Though the sun's crisply charred
entrails have slumped behind yonder peak, no one has stepped forward to claim
the amazing sum promised by the clerk. You know not one minnesinger has ever
reneged on a pledge. Until today, that is. When by the loose curtain's distracted
fall I spy the contour of an ankle, and the ferrous glint
of a meat-cleaver. Go to the judge! Tell him what you have told me
and your daughter! Implore his mercy! Then if you dare
look round to see what impression your sudden fit of sincerity hath produced.
        I'll wager you
no one leaves the room, and that the tool chest be empty! Go on! Try it! Last one in's
a rotten apple, or a—a booby. That's my last offer. Chain me to the iron bedstead

and electrocute me, so help me, that's all you're going to get out of me, harden
    my arteries
to obsidian as they will, let the mostly empty bottles
be drained till not one drop remaineth in them. Now that the killer is caught
you can return the map to Mr. Isbark.

A little loathing,
a cautious wind that pads softly
like a cat about thine loin
and argues persuasively for a cease-fire, in which one might read
much if one were wide awake and made aware, in whose bright fire
hell's thistle gleams, a league or so away. Marry, save that alibi
for your autobiography. Serve me fresh drink, I'll drink on't.
They were getting closer to your name in the list; now,
nothing will remove that stain. So how's about a walk around the old neighborhood?
Eleanor's here too. You remember Eleanor. So, nice and easy,
until it becomes something like grub, or a slug, something shapeless and horrible
you can talk back to, even scream invective at—you've got the time. And
    meanwhile our balls and
asses got to shamble on. But the daddies were keen on it.
They all liked it. Yon dork in the petting zoo,
Who, what, is it?

Two nights ago when I was complaining about all the weather we've been
    having lately,
and about how no one can do anything about it—much as I'd like to—

I was still happy, but today it turns out the drought has been secretly installed for
     weeks:
we're only beginning to feel the brunt of it. Of course, measures will be taken

but that's scarcely the point. It won't like you any better for it.
And what about mud? If we lose it, we lose everything.
Distinctions would no longer get muddied. There'd be nothing in life to wriggle
     out of,
no ooze to drop back into. We need water, heaven knows, but mud—it's so all
     over the place,
like air, that the thought of its not being there is even scarier.
Like a home that must be abandoned quickly, whose carpets and wallpaper get
     that faintly
distressed look, earth would go on without us, leave us waiting in space
for a connection that never comes. Somehow we'd survive—we always do—but
     at what cost
of mud and cosmetics. Different forms of address
would have to be adopted. Manners would become pallid, and the plot of one's life
like a thin membrane in which one can still recognize the shapes
that brought us here, and lure us on, but stronger too, to survive business,
and that would wreck our average partygoing.
I live at the bottom of the sea now.
But I can still sense a stranger
even when far off
and count the threads of partings still to be formalized.

     §

And later when we stayed talking quietly apart
in the roofless outdoor room, she had discovered
my beloved: "Well! *Improvvisatore!* It would seem God's wrath
has taken us both down a peg. I have my money. And you, I suppose, will wing it
as in the past of windy Marches and stifling Augusts we have known
together, nor regretted them once past, but say,
if not some thread, a token then, a coupon
for pats and fondlings? Was this thy gratitude for pats and fondlings,
to die like any other mortal ass?
And why, O dearest, could'st not keep thy legs,
that sacred pair, sacred to sacred me?" Why, then, risk it?
Why go after it? Anyhow, I left it in the crypt.

And all that time was much fussing, to-ing and fro-ing, and above all waiting
to see the result on the street next day. As it happened, it was a lady
in yellow, with nice legs, who turned to me and said: "Haven't you anything
    better to do?"
I wanted to cry back at her: "Yes! And these are those things! Let's
discuss your legs!" But I knew she couldn't imagine herself
filling more than the allotted space, one for her and one for herself,
so I said nothing, and she resumed her walking. *You*
understand it, though, don't you? I mean how objects, including people, can be
    one thing
and mean something else, and therefore these two are subtly disconnected? I
    don't see how
a bunch of attributes can go walking around with a coatrack labeled "person"
    loosely tied
to it with apron strings. That blows my mind. I see that you want to mean it, though.
Yes, I love it, but that doesn't mean . . .

§

A girl named Christine asked me why I have so much trouble at the office.
It's just that I don't enjoy taking orders from my inferiors, and besides,
there are so many other, nicer things to be doing! Sleeping while the navigator
is poised, adrift, and sucking each other's dicks is only one.
Travel is another. Dinard! Was ever such a place? And when you are tired
but not yet ready to return home, you can be that person again, the one who
        dragged you
here. And we made love on a car-seat
in the moonlight, except there wasn't much of it. And I was the only one!
These adventures had passed through my head while I was alone
and I thought I was having them. But you need an audience
for them to reach the third dimension. Spooks in the manor
won't do, no pre-school-age children. That night in the car, though . . .
Then we clambered down some rocks. There was a girl there who spoke of
        finance, of how
it's going to be the next most important thing. I said nothing, but wondered if I could
take my stories with me when that happens, maybe read them to others
who would appreciate them in the new financial age that offers better reception
to things of the future, like mine. False dewdrops starred her eyelashes,
and I realized we were no better off in this age than in any other, except
perhaps the Ice Age. How if we are always going to be doing things for each other
why then of course we'll miss the point, since what happens, happens off in a trailer
and we really know no more of each other than ever, and that is what
ought to be our tree, our piece of happening.
My *standing*, in the French sense of the word. How everybody accepts me
and knows they are going to see a nice sight. Forget it. None of it matters
except what I am as I am to others. Trees floating around. Hard-ons

and what to do about them. But it is arranged so that you cannot begin to play.
Knowing the rules doesn't help, in fact it's better if you don't. You have to
be *in* on it already. And if you aren't you can die very quickly, or spend the
     decades
shattered. Out of touch even with yourself.
How can I tell them that . . . or that *La Fille mal gardée* is my favorite piece of music?
I'm sorry. Look guys. In the interests of not disturbing my fragile ecological balance
I can tell you a story about something. The expression will be just right, for it
     will be adjusted
to the demands of the form, and the form itself shall be timeless though
hitherto unsuspected. It will take us down to about now,
though a few beautiful archaisms will be allowed to flutter in it—"complaint,"
for one. You will be amazed at how touched you will be because of it, yet
not tempted to find fault with the author for doing so superlative a job that it leaves
his willing but breathless readers on the sidelines, like people waiting for hours
beside a village street to see the cross-country bicycle riders come zipping through
in their yellow or silver liveries, and it's all over so fast you're not sure
you even saw it, and go home and eat a dish of plain vanilla ice cream. Noises
     that bit me,
would-be fanciers skulking around, after an autograph or a piece of your hair,
     no doubt.
And indeed there's no point in worrying about the author's tender feelings as he
     streaks along
and sees no shame in it, nor any point in your concern for his injured vanity, not
     that you don't
already love him enough, more than any writer deserves. He won't thank you for it.
But you won't mind that either, since his literature will have performed its duty
by setting you gently down in a new place and then speeding off before
you have a chance to thank it. We've got to find a new name for him. "Writer" seems
totally inadequate; yet it is writing, you read it before you knew it. And besides,

if it weren't, it wouldn't have done the unexpected and by doing so proved that
    it was quite
the thing to do, and if it happened all right for you, but wasn't the way you
thought it was going to be, why still
that is called fulfilling part of the bargain. And by doing so
he has erased your eternal debt to him. You are free. You can go now.
But the last word is always the author's so you might want to dwell a bit
more on the perfections of form adjusted to content, and vice versa too, by
    Jove! The gate
to the corral is open, and he's in there now, running around and around it
in a paroxysm of arrival that holds the attention of every last member of that
    little audience.

We're interested in the language, that you call breath,
if breath is what we are to become, and we think it is, the southpaw said.
    Throwing her
a bone sometimes, sometimes expressing, sometimes expressing something like
    mild concern, the way
has been so hollowed out by travelers it has become cavernous. It leads to death.
We know that, yet for a limited time only we wish to pluck the sunflower,
transport it from where it stood, proud, erect, under a bungalow-blue sky,
    grasping at the sun,
and bring it inside, as all others sink into the common mold. The day
had begun inauspiciously, yet improved as it went along, until at bedtime it was seen that we had prospered, I and thee.
Our early frustrated attempts at communicating were in any event long since dead.
Yet I had prayed for some civility from the air before setting out, as indeed my
    ancestors had done
and it hadn't hurt them any. And I purposely refrained from consulting *me,*

§

the *culte du moi* being a dead thing, a shambles. That's what led to me.
Early in the morning, rushing to see what has changed during the night, one
     stops to catch one's breath.
The older the presence, we now see, the more it has turned into thee
with a candle at thy side. Were I to proceed as my ancestors had done
we all might be looking around now for a place to escape from death,
for he has grown older and wiser. But if it please God to let me live until my
     name-day
I shall place bangles at the forehead of her who becomes my poetry, showing her
teeth as she smiles, like sun-stabs through raindrops. Drawing with a finger in my bed,
she explains how it was all necessary, how it was good I didn't break down on my way
to the showers, and afterwards when many were dead
who were thought to be living, the sun
came out for just a little while, and patted the sunflower

on its grizzled head. It likes me the way I am, thought the sunflower.
Therefore we all ought to concentrate on being more "me,"
for just as nobody could get along without the sun, the sun
would tumble from the heavens if we were to look up, still self-absorbed, and
     not see death.
It doesn't matter which day of the week you decide to set out on your journey. The day
will be there. And once you are off and running, it will be there still. The breath
you decide to catch comes at the far end of that day's slope, when her
vision is not so clear anymore. You say goodbye to her anyway, for the way
gleams up ahead. You don't need the day to see it by. And though millions are
     already dead

what matters is that they didn't break up the fight before I was able to get to thee,
to warn thee what would be done
to thee if more than one were found occupying the same bed.

Which is how we came to spend the night in the famous bed
that James VI of Scotland had once slept in. On its head the imperial sunflower
was inscribed, amid a shower of shooting stars. I say "imperial," though by day
he was a king like any other, only a little more decent perhaps. And next
     morning the sun
came slashing through the crimson drapes, and I was like to have died.
     Although my death
would have encouraged a few, it did not happen then, or now, and still that me
as I like to call him saunters on, caring little for the others, the past a dead
letter as far as he's concerned. So that I wrote to her
asking if *she* cared anything about the way
he was going about it, and did she know what others had done
to stop him in similar circumstances. Her reply, brought to me late at night,
     when no breath
of wind stirred in the treetops outside, caught me unawares. "If to thee

he offers neither apology nor protest, then for him it is a good thing. For thee,
on the contrary, it augurs ill. If I were thee I'd stay in bed
from dawn to evening, waiting, at least until the sun
disappears from our heavens and goes to hector those cringing in the house of
     the dead.
There can be no luck in harvest-time, no tipping of the scales, while yet he draws
     breath."

I thanked her emissary and tiptoed out without telling him what I thought of her.
How extraordinary that as soon as one settles on a plan of action, whether it be day
or darkest midnight, someone will always try to discourage you, citing death
as a possible side-effect. Yet I could not, would not, dismiss my beloved boy. No way
would I proceed along the sea with no one to bounce my ideas off of but me.
And so we two rode together. It was almost late afternoon by the time we
    reached "The Sunflower,"
as the gigantic, decaying apartment complex was named. A noted architect had done

it right once, with open spaces, communal nurseries, walkways. Yet when he
    had done,
no one liked it. People refused to move in. It was cold and impersonal. To thee,
however, it seemed a paradise. The long, alienating corridors which the sun
sliced through at regular intervals were as confusing as a casbah; the dead
tennis-courts and watchtowers seemed a present sent by death
to distract you while you waited, always for her
touch. That said, there was plenty to do at night, while during the day-
long siesta one dreamed, and brooded not, and felt fairly good. No hog's breath
stirred the rusting weeds in the little yard in front of the veranda. Like me
you too chose to put a better construction on these things than perhaps the case
    warranted; at any rate, bed
always solves everything, at least for the time being. I went out and plucked a
    sunflower
but it was empty, the birds had eaten all the seeds. Surely there's a way

to avoid feeling lonesome *and* sorry for oneself, but up until today, no way
has opened before me, I'm *both* those things, though one would suffice. What's done

is done, they say, yet I can't help wondering whether, on a different day,
you might have turned around and walked back to where I was lying face down
    in bed
and told me all the love, all the respect you had for me, that was like a shining in
    you at me,
and we could have gone off to analyze our situation and add up the particulars.
    Your breath
was your own private property, of course, and you cared little for mine, but in
    the case of her
father being in the news and so many other officials who had turned out to be dead,
perhaps in a few years' time we would have forgotten all that, to live, sunflower
and sun, in periods of rain and drought, as they do in Africa, and never fear the sun.
It is written, and played on the African thumb-piano, that those who to thee
go, and return, unremembering, are earmarked for a lonely, unpleasant death,

and those to whom thou goest never grumble, even at the prospect of death.
Therefore it is urgent that we all, pursuers and pursued, be moving in the
    common way,
for that is the only way to outwit death, none-too-clever though he may be. To thee,
I say, stand, as though on a ladder picking apricots; your back should be to the sun,
and all will pass. You'll be satisfied, you'll see. No need to shake the sunflower
husk for dried kernels. Indeed, all the grasses are long dead;
the reaching angles of the thorn-tree branches barely jerk erratically in the breath
of the savannah. If I thought for one instant that the day
of the week spelled out protection for me, or that my own misdeed would
    trickle off me
like water from a duck's back, sure and I'd have done what any decent-minded
    preacher would have done:

I'd place bunches of fresh rue and meadowsweet in glass jars filled with water
    near the bed.
I'd point with my stick not at her sins but to the shy, closed flower of her
    womanhood, her

puckered glen of swansdown, and there would have been an end to it, unless her
parents had some say in the matter. We two have lasted almost until death,
and still nothing shields us from the aspirations of the sunflower;
even at night you can hear its ever-unquiet breath
that makes of life a station on some suburban railway.
Too bad you did what you did; I, meanwhile, was lying in bed
and caught the rumble of the vans of approaching day.
"This is my day, even though it belong as well to many who are dead.
I say it not in a spirit of possessiveness, only as a fact. Indeed, I pass it to thee
as generations of aspiring lovers and writers before me have done.
Look, this is what was done to me, written on me. Take it from me."
She stood up and began to do a little dance, then as abruptly stopped, noting the sun

had passed the zenith, and was waiting to be relieved by a replacement-sun.
In all our lives I still continue to try to make headway, and though to her
what I do never makes much sense, I do it anyway, for thee.
Scratching around one is sure to uncover bits of the ancient way;
meanwhile I am reasonably well-fed, clothed and happy and spend nights in a bed
that seems beautiful to me. We used to laugh; with every breath
we'd take, some new funny thing would point a moral and adorn the day,
until at last the earth lay baking in the heat, and the sunflower

had the last laugh. "Be strong, you that are now past your prime! When you are dead
we'll talk again and see how you understand this thing men call death,
that is in reality but a shadow of what God has done
to others, to the sun and to me."

I awoke, yet I dreamed still. It seemed that all had been destined for me
all along, and as I had traveled in fear, and alone, always the sun
traveled with me. At night one sleeps in fear of wetting the bed
but he makes amends for that by pointing to our eventual death
as a teacher would point with a wand to the solution of a problem on a
        blackboard. His way
is as inscrutable as a fox's. He brings to full bloom the cornflower and the sunflower,
then lets them slip into oblivion. Why? If I knew the answer, I wouldst tell thee,
but since thou sufferest much, I'll vouchsafe that the way of the dead
is as a lightness to our dreaming, a sense of gaiety, of irresponsibility. She in her
longing realizes much, and would tell it to us, but the breath
is gone. Still, there'll come a time and not too far off when all we have done
returns to charm us; we can go back, taste, repeat it any day.

So for the moment, although tomorrow is our day,
the sun shines through the meshes. You can have me
for anything I am, or want to be, and I'll replace you with me, introduce you to
        the sun.
When summer calls, and people wish they only had a way,
and nights are too thick, and days have barely begun to be spoiled, I'll riddle thee
about what we heard before we came here, how much is already done.
The moral of the story however is that the ubiquitous sunflower

knows the secret and cares. As a door on its hinges, so he in his bed
turns and turns, and in his turning unlocks the rusted padlock of death,
that flies apart and at once I am shriven. Take me in, teach me her
ways, but above all don't leave me for dead:
I live, though I draw only a little breath.

The story that she told me simmers in me still, though she is dead
these several months, lying as on a bed. The things we used to do, I to thee,
thou to me, matter still, but the sun points the way inexorably to death,
though it be but his, not our way. Funny the way the sun
can bring you around to her. And as you pause for breath,
remember it, now that it is done, and seeds flare in the sunflower.

And left it that way, and then it kind of got shelved. It was a missing increment,
but as long as no one realized it was missing, calm prevailed. When they did, it
    was well
on the way to being a back number of itself. So while people cared, and some
    even wept,
it was realized that this was a classic, even a generic, case, and soon
they called attention to other aspects of the affair. No one ever explained how a
    trained
competitor of long standing would just bar itself from the case that way, there
    being no
evidence of self-interest, except insofar as loving a sun constitutes one. They
    shied away
from this one, and it was with no love
or self-pity in its heart that it betook itself then down the few stone steps leading

to the crypt. Here, at least, peace of a sort reigned, better than the indifferent bog
of schnorrers and nay-sayers it had kept company with for so long, a whole
    season, and the unlovely
atmosphere that had soured that season at its close was not recognized here: it
    was a currency
no one had any use for. If this left one like sailcloth, with the grained and toned
texture of one who has seen much, and still wishes to help, why all the better:
    one could go
farther and fare worse than entertain the possibility of such a journey, a *voyage
    d'affaires*
that will consistently be fun at any given moment. And so, though stalks heavy
    with the
mothy, mopheaded bloom may tremble next August, that is a thing of the past; the sun
purges its mind of all negative thoughts, granting
equanimity with the largesse of one who has too much, and
causes people to re-examine their attitudes. Maybe get some rain?
Are sherbets more glorious now than formerly? So this small, piecemeal
    uncurling exposes
vast sheets of preoccupations that the sun's firmness can in many cases
cause to evaporate before their expiration date. A hound-shaped fragment of
    cloud rises
abruptly to the impressive center of the heavens only to fold itself
behind itself and fade into the distance even as it advances
bearing news of the channel coast. That is the archetypal kind of development
we're interested in here at the window girls move past continually. Something
must be happening beyond the point where they turn
and become mere fragments. But to find out what that is,
we should be forced to relinquish this vantage point, so
deeply fought for, hardly won.

Yes, others chorused, and
we'll see to it that good use is made of it once they find you. Sea
so dark, O harvester, is it possible they could have brought you and me together
after so long, only to be separated in an instant? There must have been some
    purpose to this,
some idea hiding in the vacuity, the regular oblongs that comprise
your adverse assessment of my capabilities, like building blocks? But no,
it says, please sit down, you're upsetting the others. With my cant,
my stammer, I suppose? Oh all right, I'll go peaceably, but when you next see me,
rigged out in nickel armor to do battle with the henchpersons—it doesn't matter
whose—you'll descry in me a note of alarming mildness that I was saving
for just such an occasion. After all, *I*
can go on living here, and I don't mind emptiness, but you
must fill your days with satisfying chatter. Then, just as the moon's cloak
grazes the tits of some remote foothills, we'll engage
each other constructively, your energy will flow into me and vice versa, and behold,
all will have been in vain, the warring, the contusions, the peacemongering:
we'll have only ourselves, and only ourselves to blame.

§

Excellent is the peach, and stirring the tales
of battle, the calls to emulation. But excellent also is the spat-out pit, the ideal
of zero growth, when it comes to that. I think all men should argue, and then
      give in, for it
takes time to really make up one's mind about certain matters. Days of
      mourning
in particular.

Then when somebody comes to ask you if you have freshened up, or would like to,
the whole freight train of associations is set in motion, lumbers gracelessly
along the clacking tracks, and it isn't so much as if you *had* made up your mind,
      indeed
had done so quite some time ago, thank you, but as if it's all off
and running: the race to the pageant, stiff competition among the ushers,
the stagehands. And now I want it to be the way
it was. I'm very particular about the trivia I associate with,
but for which I'd long ago have passed out from boredom. Which brings me to
      you: how do *you*
like it, and could you care if you saw a sample of it escaping from the mass
to go inform other, unenlightened souls of whom we spoke and thought were past
redemption and caring but who shine like the night breezes
in this direction, the dew on them is genuine, and are those
tears? Who said it that way? I'll go another way. And she'll have me
then, there'll be no recourse, and we shall be happy after all, that's all there is to
      it, you'll
see.

      §

It will never make any difference now, but
it remains to note how the change will affect your work. Empty slots in the zodiac
presage no good, nor the giant pebble at its center, but who knows, with patience
and a little hunger one makes one's way. From here you can see the town,
bustling with various kinds of sleepy activity. Old trucks in the squares.
Above it a few celestial blips, comparing different depths in space, how it feels
against a sky of tinfoil, and seemingly just emptied, but it has always been thus.
Gradually, heads appear around the rim of the crater, blotted in the sunlight.
Just gentle, happy suds, and the time to be missing:
all the time in the world, he liked to say,
and I'd recriminate too if I had escaped but it's not clear that I have. I stumbled
into an abandoned pigpen just now, and they are watching, which is all
anybody ever does. If I had books here I'd read.

Characterizing this rebuttal as "hogwash," the senator strode swiftly through the
    marble rotunda,
commenting the day's happenings without missing a beat. We have seen that the
    police
charge you more for delivering a baby when it's clement outdoors. We have seen
signs of life in the land of waiting, but it's too soon to rejoice; we'll
let you know. Others may have been after him to unzip the course, which
    wouldn't explain
dance orchestras in the rainy plaza or the unquestioning look of one child whose doll
came in second. In the hayloft the air was pure and fresh
and I could remember how once all of existence was as painfully expectant,
    careless of duration
as the mayflies trying to just get by, and how this curdled at evening with the
    smell of socks

and underarm deodorant so that that desperate patch seemed a nice place to be.
    Anyway it
had tested our mettle, whatever that is. Warnings boiled up seemingly out of the
    ground
but it was difficult to know what to make of them, or even to know who they
    were meant for.
Was it the last train? No pass to the way home from school? It was hard too to
    decode the missing,
who had apparently been seen as recently as this morning, turning away after
    being turned away.
Their locks are always a little more opalescent, their gussets straighter. Hygiene
is always a problem in the jungle, but you can stay here for decades and never appear
flushed, or flustered. Something about the thinness of the topsoil. They stand you
up and march you away and nobody looks afraid, just bored, and the majesty of
    the larkspur
performs annually. Refreshments are on a first-come, first-served basis. We have
    seen the cage
and the humdrum animals it contains. We have seen the house of the leader,
a little farther off. And the numbered apples on his trees.
It can never be anything but symbolic.
By that I mean it can never cause utterance in outsiders,
only second thoughts and self-doubt. For the discourse (and by discourse I mean
    lively discourse)
to take place on a meaningful level, that is, outside someone's brain, a state of artificial
sleep would have to be induced, first of all. Then the skills for measuring reflexive
response would have to be sharply honed. Finally, the patient's automatic, and
    therefore healthy,
impulse toward duplicity would have to be sorted out, strand by strand, in order
    that the
viable negative attempts to ward off phenomena like the empurpled dais of the
    approaching

twilit gloom might be measured, both as to sincerity and effectiveness. This
    technically
not unrealizable state of affairs would then bring us closer, but only a little, to a
    vantage
point from which the abiding, negative (but in the sense of "passive") sheathing
    of the soul might
offer an overview of what might be mounted inside that, but the view our
    telescope afforded
would be that of an episode which happened several trillion light-years ago, a fleeting
one at that, a grace-note in some cosmic oratorio from which one would then try
    to extrapolate
a sense of all that comes after, and how it jibes with the average mind of today,
its feeding habits, outbursts, and so on. The attempt is certainly worth making, even
if it only corroborates the central dark thesis about the purely symbolic, anti-
    functional
nature of the universe as a setting for the countless doomed initiatives that flourish
in it to supply compost for the core-concept, a somewhat antiquated but still
    functioning
regulatory system that organizes us in some semblance of order, binding some of
    us loosely,
baling others of us together like straw, but always there is a connection, albeit
    sometimes an
extremely loose one like a tendril that brushes against one, a lock of hair that
    falls over
the eye or a buzzing insect that is never too far away. And though the armature
that supports all these varied and indeed desperate initiatives has begun
to exhibit signs of metal fatigue it is nonetheless sound and beautiful in its
    capacity to perform
functions and imagine new ones when appropriate, the best model anyone has
    thought up
so far, like a poplar that bends and bends and is always capable of straightening itself

after the wind has gone; in short it is my home, and you are welcome in it
for as long as you wish to stay and abide by the rules. Still,
the doubling impulse that draws me toward it like some insane sexual attraction can
not be realized here. For that to take shape one would have to be able to
     conceive a linear
space independent of laws in which blunted gestures toward communication
     could advance or recede
without actually moving from the spot to which they are rooted; in other words,
     destiny could
happen all the time, vanish or repeat itself ad infinitum, and no one would be
     affected, one's
real interests being points that define us, the line, which is dimensionless and
     without desire.
Thus, all things would happen simultaneously and on the same plane, and
     existence, freed
from the chain of causality, could work on important projects unconnected to
     itself and so
conceive a new architecture that would be nowhere, a hunger for nothing, desire
     desiring itself,
play organized according to theology with a cut-off date, before large façades.
     And these
urges, if that's what they are, would exist already without propriety, without the need
or possibility of fulfillment, what the bass clarinet is to the orchestra, though of
     course we
would all get along very much as we do now, since human perfectibility would not
be sacrificed but on the contrary get promoted to the first desk, where it belongs,
and everybody would be free to draw his or her own conclusions and take them
     home like homework
provided the constellations remained inalterable, which is another question, and the
concept of beauty were abolished, which is another and possibly more important
     one. Anyway,

it looks like a nice day for all this, and I invite you to start revving up your VCR's;
who knows what may happen? In the meantime, look sharp, and sharply at
    what is around you; there is
always the possibility something may come of something, and that is our
fondest wish though it says here I'm not supposed to say so, not now, not
in this place of wood and sunlight, this stable or retiring room or whatever you
    want to call it.

Excuse me while I fart. There, that's better. I actually feel relieved.

Who knew at the time how froward they would be
later on, and in what circumstances we would be meeting again,
and how others with the names of heroes of boys' adventure novels would be
    replacing us
on the perilously steep escalator of destiny that only lurches upward,
ever unsatisfied, forever finding fault? Some of this crowd
were about right. But it can never stop raining. There are places you drive through
and people who come out to see what's going on, but in the end these are effects
merely. The truly vitiated look haggard and mean, whether they be socially
acceptable or no, and still the perquisite authority hasn't been distilled;
it is everyone's, for everyone to see. I will show you fear in a handful of
    specialists. Furthermore
the burliest male is but as a handmaiden to the suspicion of his own history:
he's got it right, OK? And so have a few others, while the waiting's been going
    on. But enough of
this self-congratulation in Aegean sunrises. Who are we, after all? And who
    needs profundity?

The moment I came down here I knew it was going to get better. There were
        autographs to sign,
and contracts, many of them in sextuplicate, and so I knew I was in for a good rest
after a long drive, and they'd leave me in peace, though not forget about me. Alas,
how sparsely furnished it all looks now. Chatterton's garret? And how much
        harder it is to pinpoint
the single, modestly important thing, now that we know its freight would be
long in coming, and much harder to decipher than any
entity before now. But of course! That's the solution! We know ourselves and
        everything
of the past. The one thing we don't know is how silly it's going to look in about five
minutes, like an eighteenth-century cherub atop a globe. You fuck me, I'll
fix you. You give me that, and I'll give you this. It's all so important yet so
        excruciatingly
banal, isn't it, darling? Then we'll have come home and there will be an end to it,
and they that have found it already shall have it taken away from them, and we who
never knew what a good thing we were on to shall be reproached and rewarded
with the viceroy's attention, though we must stand outside, I think. Fortify my
        ignorance
then, I shan't be doing anything to anybody but must not for this
reason stand alone, uninspired by hope. Three seasons shall pass before anybody
        gets up the nerve to jump,
by which time a perverse
order shall reign and those who have inspired us shall take their places in it
like latecomers ushered to their seats at the opera once the overture is finished.
        You can't
can it and sell it, that's for sure, but it *is* a commodity, and someday all
will be wiser for it. And the paradoxically strong sense of personal loss that
        overwhelms you
when you hear about the death of someone you barely knew will answer for it
        too: you'll

be exonerated and no one will ever make fun of you again, or turn aside
when your name is mentioned. Meanwhile you'll be slightly happy when they
see how much your standing in this rigid matriarchal society has been enhanced
by the little you do, trying to scrape out a living and keeping your sense of humor,
which is, assuredly, not always easy. Anyway, someone will care.
They'd better. And the funk take over. The generations collapse like floors
in a burning building, and it will all somehow be . . . *appropriate*. Er, yes. We is rich
and handsome, as it were. HOWEVER,
I'll face the world alone. Bad cats will want to eat me. Autos
will run over me. Dogs will chase me. Chickens, hawks, tigers, lions . . . Perhaps
I'd better ride up with you. You understand, of course.
I certainly don't want to live next to a taxidermist. Miss Gale, I may need you later.

Then in the car he proposed to me. In the back seat. We drank sacrificial wine.
It was so *good*. And underneath I was saying,
all men are rogues, but I guess I like them,
if that's what they are. Then we went out and a cloud like a magician's cape
covered the sun. I'll never forget that. And we walked on
awhile and I was trying to explain my embarrassing
tendency not to be able to distinguish things that happened to me years ago
from recent dreams. He was cool for a while after that. Men
never seem to know how much to erase, and afterward it's bedlam, greed and
        self-interest take over
to a point where they actually cancel each other out, and one is left
hungry for one's greed, at least it was something, and now, why no
one has anything left to be impatient about. It's like damp weather.

§

And everybody said no wonder. It's an hour to find you.
You, so belated in the past, your comments could never be
interpreted as part of history, or so you said, and that's what we thought.
I'm just a copier. You are the history, the book. In time I think
it'll get you straight and all peoples will see what we're up to. In the past they
      chided you:
no more. I'm sending for your things, your books and things, we'll go over
it again in the morning. First get a good night's sleep. There are people who
      think nothing of
writing out a check for the full amount and handing it to you. I mean we're talking
debts canceled, a link to the future, daybreak . . . Well I thought so too and
still I've had it with those who want to own you, as it were,
and give you nothing in return. Still, if it were possible to come to some
      agreement
or other, I think I'd be content, and they too. Here, it says in the bar
how much we're going to spend, and then we'll be equidistant from base camp
      and the
summit and have some voice in our lives and how much the future matters
to us, and to others as well. Boy, I'll say so. Meanwhile, do you
think they're going to kill us in cold blood? Naw, I don't think so, besides
it's too risky, and we're on this side of the great river, they
on the other. I'd like to thank you for what you just said, but I could never
find the words.

Oh, that's all right.

   §

A soft rain,
a sudden shower. Why shouldn't it?
And of all the ones I like
this is the most promising. Here in the dry
it is, anyway. It likes us, saying, "We'll get you over
this one, then hand you back the tiller. The others
are all love and lovers, sometimes." We won't bite,
though, having been deceived so often in the past. The fact that the
happy ending's only waiting your approval dooms it; you shall go off the deep end
once more and ultimately, and, not to put too fine a deconstruction on it, be
    redeemed only
in a distant future no one cares to look into. There's so much of it going round
now that no one wants to look farther than his or her pocket mirror. It's funny
    how certain natural
calamities bring people together at times, separate them at others. Rampant "me
    tooism"'s certainly
the order of the day, and such a tall order; one can view oneself framed,
    silhouetted, dead, and
still only think in terms of surfaces, boundaries; the very heavens
have lifted off for destinations unknown, and as we can sit
here, we do. It isn't uncold. Whence comes Iceland's beam? But suppose you
    know someone who's
got a vested interest, an urge to show you how your hostility is what's aborting
the final, suave wrap-up, with the guts to stand up and say so—*then*
aren't we uniting, and isn't something due
to come of it when the last tears stain the oak flooring, and the roasted
    swans, the pineapples,
are sent away untasted. How many of us does *that* make?
Two, surely, but there is something like flowers in the room, and that makes it
a magic number, confounding calculations, canceling reports,

bringing in other unknown elements that are a form of art, at least
as long as they stay that way. True, that puts us in one another's way; we can no
    longer
aim at that destination on the wall, that hill outside the window, that seemed to
    promise
indefinite relief, but at least, being boxed in, can thwart the unknown at home,
    swear
fidelity and probably mean it this time. And meanwhile the tottering parade of
    ancient red
double-decker London buses winds past the window like a shriek
of victory but in reality contradicting itself: no carnival could be this atrocious *and*
unfrequented, at least it seems so to me. And one fits exactly the space of the mind
opposite one; there is no
sequel and no blank pages. As far as I'm concerned it's a draw, and a decent one
    at that
if you keep your mind off it.

Voices of autumn in full, heavy summer;
algae spangling a pool. A lot remains to be done, doesn't it?
I haven't even begun to turn myself inside-out yet, and that
has to precede even an informal beginning. Try making up those childish
    itineraries we were once
so apt at, and you'll see. Even my diary has become an omen to me,
and I know how I'll have to go on writing it; it would be disappointed
otherwise. And those days we have to get through! Afternoons at the store,
and when bluish evening, the color of television
in a window high above the street, comes on, who has the strength to
judge it all according to a pre-existing set of criteria and then live with it,
let alone enjoy it and aim it at being a force for good, in one's life and that of those

we share, for a time, this earth with, and later on to judge the after-effect of those
        fruits of it
which may no longer exist except as examples and increasingly dim ones at that? Why,
it's enough to make you want to leave home, strike out on your own
at midnight: "Why Girls Leave Home," "The Trial of Mary Dugan": maybe
        these were the things
they were saying then in the theater or writing about in novels so that
people would *understand* and thereby save themselves a lot of trouble
and floundering. In the unprincipled mire we walk about in today, nobody
        bothers even
to warn you about the perils of white slavery (to cite an extreme example), but
        then again
nobody is forcing you to save yourself either. That would be uncouth. Yet it
        would be nice
to think that years afterward one might have a good laugh about it,
and that assurance is precisely what we lack today. The fact is that no one even cares
what's it all about. They see only shoe-leather
thinning into the future, and the inexorable dawn
shading into dusk, and know that's what they're made of, like it
or not. That's what everybody's made of,
and it comes as no shock to find out that the present is, after all, brittle
as glass in a burning conservatory. Listening to the dance music from outside
is all that matters. Really. Stockings are of secondary importance.

There was a strange, scorched taste to the soup,
I thought. Had you?

§

Otherwise who would believe us when we came
home to taste the soup, and cry a little, not wanting much?
Like little girls pretending to understand each other
when they talk like adults, we'd see that living
on this alternate rail was possible but not
eminently desirable, though definitely possible.

O in that winter what tore my thought was the shiny poem
I was about to read and recite, and write: a lacquered thing
with an even more exciting nimbus that spelt out possibilities
in all the tales we were going to be told, all the wrongs
inflicted on us and in turn by us on all those
around us, neither more nor less fortunate than we.

Trying to drum up business one begins explaining recklessly
one's family and the dates in one's house, the little
plum tree visible in the enclosure. The path one made
forcing oneself. And now these are out of date and exactly what is
required here. Let's pass on them without analyzing them,
and others who sang here, knowing justice mysterious, and out of the way,

the way a moth sings in the house. A letting go,
as finger by finger unclasps. But we told it the way we wanted it to go.
So what about your story? And the fires that made you, better

than you wanted, still not worth dying for? I placed an ad,
it was wrong of me, and how should I go?

There—it's over. And what a blessed relief. I have always loved the
sight of women sewing, and holly at the eaves, sometimes a look that
spears you through the darkness: you are the unaccountable one
but there are acres of us just now. And I thought I came off looking lewd.
No, but with the dock ahead, and that man in pinstripes
and bowler. We knew there'd be repercussions, but they were soft
as cotton candy when they came, and respectful, like dreams
put away, like money in the bank.

Time was when weather seemed a release. Today it's screwed down
all the way, like a cap on a jar, yet it mirrors something
in each one of us, something we had been trying to find out
without much success as dogs came and went across
dull afternoons—the "dear, dead days" as someone called them.

It's there, but with a new intensity. Everything is landscaped
for one's greater peace of mind, the furnaces within banked
for greater authoritativeness. I would like to
come out on the plus side, *it* wants us to, and amid the
explosions of careless lovemaking I suppose that's possible.
What's the catch? No doubt it lies somewhere along the way

§

of overreacting to these minute meteorological changes,
a slight twist to the horizon's lip or the ghost
of a frown that could have seen anything, such as the V of a bird
disappearing desultorily into a cloud. And meanwhile
there are rooms to be put back in order.

How does one explain that by never looking back one is always
seeing backward, into the scarves, the times that never were,
and that placing one foot before the other is only a sign
to the unconscious guides to follow, and that one's destination
is the empty stockade, not this crowded landing? So it is when children

forget to grow and they are suddenly looking at being older,
not recognizing much? Or when people decide to migrate
from the village that has held them all these years like a spot
and uncomplainingly releases them to fall back
into the dreams that are the very fabric of our maturing,
now that we've got one, assuming it's still there, on permanent loan?

The sound the water made
when I brushed my teeth seemed a good idea. Later the sources
became clear, as in a picture. There was nobody to go to that day.

Yet as long as the pins held, here was where I
would someday be—no kidding. And O I
held you through the long winter, held to you.

The numismatic triumphs, the snakes and ladders
of outrageous fortune were what finally put us across,
its message. And some days the wind does blow heavier
but it's with special understanding for our case, those inverted commas
without which we can't function it seems.

An odor of big bands in the night and one stands up,
free to go. If ever they
came looking for us, this is where we'd be. And who doesn't want to be right here?
Yes, the more I think about it. We're going to stay. We've elected to.
Pass the celery.

Then the travel came at him. You know what I mean.
A last chance to air the old mass. Going home, after so many promises
to consult the self before the next spin. It erodes. We all had a chance
at the city of faces moving around. Now it's humdrum detection
from a many-sided tower on which we interact,
perhaps. And this neck of the woods is picked over.
After a rain the slattern light spreads again
creating all endeavors like ditches that only spread
farther into the trees and eyesight as my wrenched narrative drips on, decays

while some sing of the heart and a few, in a home, of lasting walls
or winds, and live in and love the riddle that proposes us.

Also by seacoast moles the wave gives up the ship, slams
it against the slip. We are in more heartfelt times now that
vacancy defines itself, that true aether. Conversely the body lines
"evanish all, like vapours in the air," burnish the curve or cove
at certain times seen as majestic, or merely at rest, a timeless,
unwired mood from which good can fall. And chiefly does. Though I am aware
of a moaning under the door, a secret treaty, plans to shanghai the settled
order during the night when we are awake and cold, losing the thread.
This said, the bauble that peace sprouted, is
it another camp collectible, or are its strings somehow
drawn too taut in us? Then the next thing explodes,
like a cigar or a vase of flowers. Left in the rubbery wake one still keeps
meaning to be around both before and after, not during necessarily,
since there is no fruitful rest there, only a game of opposites posing
as right for the happy-to-be-blind and the tense modifiers,
grouping. All along that stand of trees you shed a path
adjacent to the end and some grazed there, mooring
large questions of how do you get off and what are we waiting for? Standing
like this? When all of spring is away? Who do you get to change it?

You take a guy who's never seen one before, a weather like this, and perforce he
will deduce brightnesses out of the pervading dullness we never knew were there;
it becomes a construction. So that the later glare of tidings seems almost "natural,"
and the agreement that hands closed on, a bargain, in that time and place.

§

Suddenly they all stopped talking about it. Yet I
can't get it out of my head. I just saw it here somewhere
late last evening. As a result, nobody thinks I'm normal, but I don't
care. Every answer may have been salted and put away just so as to spoil,
like a dissertation of some kind. A great deal of thinking went into it and out
    the other side.

But I did want to get back to the personal barbs. Why was I wailing for them?
Fact: people leave their doors open and don't even flush the toilet.
Fact: loving one another in these parts is more like gunboat diplomacy than it is
like a soap opera, and I, who don't care, always get caught in the middle.
I belong there anyway. I'm going to someplace from someplace, and think in
    these terms.
I'm like a corset string that gets laced up but never tied. I've tried to be kind and
    helpful,
I know I have, but this is about something else. It's about me. And so I am never
off the hook; I look at others and reflect their embarrassed, sheepish grin: all right,
can I go home now? But I know deep in my heart of hearts I never will, will
    never want to,
that is, because I've too much respect for the junk we call living
that keeps passing by. Still, I might be tempted
to love or something if the right person came along, or the time were right;
I know I would. But I can't be tempted, so far. I'm too pure, like the nature
of temptation itself, and meantime the fans stand back and wonder what to
    admonish
the players with, and I sit here empty-handed, my breast teeming

with unexplained desires and acrostics. I'll go on like this. Take my glasses off.
And he says to me, I'll vote for you. Our roads are poor. And he laughed and said it.

Others were paying for this call which is why in the first place
no string of dignity remained, no mention of how they would reopen
the clogged career of someone just starting out in life who finds himself injured
and cannot explain why. There is blood everywhere—no wound,
just the sign of bleeding. If one had thought not to count
and tabulate every moment and expose it to the litmus of living in some way
I can't understand, then it would be all right for those bald men at the beach and
     some could
redeem the morning pledge and saunter off distractedly into the football fields
of dusk, and leave others alone, and welcome death as a diversion and they in
     turn could write
this down. Lakes and raccoons and unspotted moons would be the result.
As it is, everyone now finds himself inferior: repeat, everyone.
There is unrest; the shadow of the ball carries over.
I am left to repeat standards that have no particular relevance for me. I write
on the sides of buildings and on the backs of vehicles, and still
no nail divides the splinter from its neighbor, no fish swims close to another.
I have seen it all, and I write, and I have seen nothing.

Draw up a map right now—all of the notches are there.
If we cared like this it would be all right, wouldn't it, so why
doesn't somebody do something? In addition to which God doesn't want us to
     be stupid
or overreact, else why these chains? *We don't have much call for those.* We can

slip into the forest with it, and be bait. I know I'd be taking off nothing
if I let you believe otherwise, but it's all I can do. The season is even rude
to finish us off, but there is something we have to do, weather permitting,
across the street before the king is murdered.
Anyway, it was the commandant's word against mine.

The incubus awoke from a long, refreshing sleep.
A lot of people think they have only to imagine a siren for it to exist,
that the truth in fairy tales is somehow going to say them. I tend to agree
with dumb people who intervene, and are lost; actors of a different weakness
who explain the traceries of fallen leaves as models for our burgeoning etiquette,
a system that doesn't let us off the hook as long as we are truth and know it,
the great swing of things. And of course it may yet turn up.

I couldn't believe he said it. But that's the way we lived. It existed.
I've been at this stand for years and I think I see how the wool
is pulled over our eyes gradually, so that each of us thinks of ourselves as falling
    asleep
before it happens, then wakes to a pang of guilt: was it that other me again?
Why did I take my mind off the roast, as it turned
hypnotically on its spit, and now it's charred beyond recognition?

The multiplication of everything ran on years back, she said,
until two scraps had been assembled. Then it was up to the death-rattle.
There was a great conflict at that time.

There are canisters of cartridges from that era which do little to dispel
the legend of our rabid ancestors. Hey,
they're yours as well as mine, buster.
Yet once the funeral herbs were strewn there was peace of a sort. The evergreen
canopy became an anagram of itself, telling us much
about how gold was hidden in the old places, and spirits that came forth, irritated,
from their resting place and pulled the magic latch-string, and the door flew open
and there were the wolf and Red Riding Hood in bed together, except that the wolf
was really Grandma. Whew! What a relief! They don't write them that way
        anymore,
because the past is overlay. What a city this is! In what rich though tepid layers
        you can
almost detect the outline of your head and then
you know it's time to read on. When crisis comes, with embraceable side-effects,
let's put a roof on the thing before it sidles, world-bound,
toward an unconvincing other world. I'm more someone else, taking dictation
from on high, in a purgatory of words, but I still think I shall be the same person
        when I get up
to leave, and then repeat the formulas that have come to us so many times
in the past ("It's softer"), so faithfully that we extend them
like a sill, and they have an end, though a potentially hazardous one,
though that's about all we can do about it. Every film is an abidance. We are
        merely agents, so
that if something wants to improve on us, that's fine, but we are always the last
to find out about it, and live up to that image of ourselves as it gets
projected on trees and vine-coated walls and vapors in the night sky: a distant
noise of celebration, forever off-limits. By evening the traffic has begun
again in earnest, color-coded. It's open: the bridge, that way.

A Note About the Author

John Ashbery is the author of thirteen previous books
of poetry, including *April Galleons* (1987), and of a
volume of art criticism, *Reported Sightings* (1989).
His *Self-Portrait in a Convex Mirror* received the
Pulitzer Prize for poetry, as well as the National Book
Critics Circle Award and the National Book Award.
He has been named a Guggenheim Fellow and a Mac-
Arthur Fellow, and is a chancellor of the Academy
of American Poets. In 1989–90 he was Charles Eliot
Norton Professor of Poetry at Harvard. He is cur-
rently Charles P. Stevenson, Jr. Professor of Literature
at Bard College.

A Note on the Type

This book was set on the Linotype in Granjon, a type named in compliment to Robert Granjon, a type cutter and printer active, in Antwerp, Lyons, Rome, and Paris, from 1523 to 1590. Granjon, the boldest and most original designer of his time, was one of the first to practice the trade of type founder apart from that of printer.

Linotype Granjon was designed by George W. Jones, who based his drawings on a face used by Claude Garamond (c. 1480–1561) in his beautiful French books. Granjon more closely resembles Garamond's own type than does any of the various modern faces that bear his name.

Composed by Heritage Printers, Inc., Charlotte, North Carolina. Printed and bound by Halliday Lithographers, West Hanover, Massachusetts.

Designed by Anthea Lingeman.